This book is the opposite of *Leadership for Dummies* ... This is the bible for intelligent, committed leaders who want to make a difference. Michelle has gained the wisdom in these pages the hard way, through decades on the front line as a therapist, leader and organisational consultant. This wisdom is backed up by the latest science to guide you to lead yourself, your team and your organisation and to create a psychologically safe climate where everyone can be their best. This is a book that will change you and your organisation forever.

Peter Cook, Chairperson at Thought Leaders

As a leader, if you want to reach your potential, create high performing teams and foster a great workplace culture then you must read this book. Michelle Bihary draws on her vast education, knowledge and experience to provide such valuable insights and practical information to effectively lead above the line.

Debbie Gabreal, Head of Customer Relations at QBE

Leading Above the Line provides a very thought-provoking look at how our behaviours as leaders can have a profound ripple effect throughout an organisation. Ensuring we lead ourselves is pivotal to bringing out the best in our teams. Anyone in a leadership role will find useful information in Michelle's book, which gives a clear framework on how to achieve a healthy culture.

Paul Greenhalgh, Chief Executive Officer at South Gippsland Hospital

It's a challenge to consistently bring your best self to the workplace. *Leading Above the Line* provides a structured and considered approach that brings theory to life to help you create an environment where you, and your team, can thrive and hit peak performance. Never has it been more important to think about your impact and lead with intention. *Leading Above the Line* is a great place to start.

Cynthia Gebert, CEO, Energy and Water Ombudsman (Victoria)

In this book, Michelle presents a game-changing framework to create a harmonious and high achieving workplace. She has applied leading edge neuroscience to leadership and made it accessible and practical. And it works. This book is my everyday go-to for big picture leadership strategies towards whole-of-practice wellbeing. As a result, creativity, productivity and teamwork have flourished in our practice. I wish I had found Michelle and her work 20 years ago.

**Robyn Stephen, Director and Principal Clinician
at Melbourne Child Development**

An extraordinary contribution to leadership literature and an essential read for all leaders seeking to foster trust and psychological safety in their workplace. Michelle's insights provide a road map for leaders to create and nurture interpersonal relationships and an environment where individuals, teams and organisations can thrive. There has never been a more critical time for leaders to step up and 'show themselves' and their humanity. Thank you, Michelle.

Jenni Richardson, Client Services Director

Michelle generously shares her knowledge and considerable expertise in leadership in this exciting new book. The book brings together science and the aspects we all need in order to self-lead and lead others in a readable and enjoyable format. I applaud Michelle for bringing this excellent information to all of us. The human need for safety, to feel valued, to be fulfilled and to have connections in our work lives are explained. The difficulties of managing work-life balance are expertly dismantled for the reader. The inextricable influence of environments, particularly work environments, on how we feel, what we do and how we work reminds me of Michelle's professional underpinnings in occupational therapy. Plus the abundance of professional expertise is evident as Michelle takes us above the line. Well done, Michelle.

Helen Bourke-Taylor, Associate Professor at Monash University

I have known and benefited from Michelle's work for many years and across multiple human service organisations. For myself and the teams I've led, this work has been transformative. Michelle has amassed a body of wisdom that crosses disciplines, traverses contemporary challenges and seeks to find new and enabling paradigms. In this book, you will find invitations to challenge yourself, gain greater self-mastery and ultimately find your true north as a leader. If there is one thing our world and our systems are lacking at this moment of global reckoning, it is genuine leadership. I hope that you will accept the invitations contained within these pages and step into your own power to lead above the line.

Faorligh Hunter, Regional Director at Berry Street

The current pandemic represents an opportunity to genuinely change how we operate as individuals and at our places of work. In this book, Michelle's broad experience combined with sound evidence forms a recipe that allows individuals to explore, grow and enhance their potential—benefiting every aspect of their lives. Michelle provides you with the tools to construct a deeper understanding of how to lead yourself above the line—flowing through to positively influencing workplace culture and thus workplace outcomes.

Michael Falloon, Healthcare Leader

Michelle has written a high-quality book on inspirational leadership; her insights and strategic advice about leadership are transforming. Michelle is informed by psychological insights, neuroscience research, understandings about emotional intelligence, mental health awareness and a deep knowledge that emanates from her years of experience as a mental health practitioner and trainer of teams in a myriad of work environments. This book will help leaders thrive and build a productive environment where employees feel safe enough to put their minds, hearts and souls into their work.

Ms. Anastasia Panayiotidis, General Manager of Clinical Services at Relationships Australia, Victoria

As I read this book, I found myself saying ' Yes and yes and yes' many times. It is clearly and articulately written and the concept of 'leading above the line' will resonate with anyone who has been a manager or has been managed well or badly. I can't wait to put the concepts into action. So much of this resonates with me having been part of wonderful teams with a superb leader for many years and then having the experience of a micromanager director that undermined the team, including myself, to the extent that I lost all confidence in my skills and abilities. I will use and recommend this book to peers and colleagues as we work together through the pandemic, when more than ever good leadership in health is fundamentally important.

Dr Samantha Colquhoun, International Health Research Fellow and Epidemiologist at the Australian National University

Team performance is inextricably linked to the human condition— our people can only do their best work when they are their best selves. This means that leaders must be comfortable looking beyond the concrete stuff of goals and actions, and navigate the much messier world of culture, relationships and human psychology. I can't imagine a better person than Michelle to equip leaders with these skills.

Simon Dowling, Leadership Mentor and Author of *Work with me: How to get people to buy into your ideas*

The timely release of *Leading Above the Line* guides us to re-examine the workplace climate, how we function as leaders and how we lead others. I feel I've gained renewed energy to champion for systemic change towards workplace environments that support us to function at our best. As we enter this new era, I believe the wisdom Michelle offers on leadership lays a strong foundation for what we wish to become and what we wish to contribute.

Joan Leo, Allied Health Educator at Mercy Health

This book is a game changer. Its launch is perfectly timed amid the chaos of understanding and dealing with COVID times when many of us are re-evaluating not only our own future, but that of our workplaces. The mix of theory, practical examples and reflective questions enable you to learn, develop and embed positive change to lead with confidence.

Randa Abbasi, Occupational Therapist and Health Leader at WorkSpace IQ, NZ

This book is a timely, welcome resource for leaders in what has become a very uncertain and threatening world. Leading above the line is harder, yet more important. Thanks so much to Michelle for providing this evidence-based, insightful and practical guide to help leaders thrive, despite the challenges. When leaders understand there is a line and know how to stay above it, they help lift others up to do the same. *Leading Above the Line* provides an inspiring vision for our future world of work.

Karen Morley, Executive Coach, Author and Speaker

A must-have book for every leader trying to navigate these challenging times. Michelle's work is crucial for creating a powerful leadership mindset, taking the lead for the team and supporting others to lead themselves.

Jane Anderson, Strategic Communication Expert at Jane Anderson Communications

Now more than ever, leaders need a road map to design a better workplace. Michelle has delivered this in *Leading Above the Line*. Firmly grounded in neuroscience, her ideas will help leaders and teams create the workplaces of the future.

Rebecca Bradshaw, Author of *Decide, Design, Delegate*

The depth of Michelle's experience has led to the creation of this caring and pragmatic reflection on the need for change in our workplace. She draws a line in the sand challenging leaders to step up to the interpersonal and structural opportunities that will create healthy organisations. This book is a cri de coeur for creating the kind of workplace where human beings thrive and ultimately build the success of the business and community.

Gayle Smerdon PhD

I urge any leader, in fact, anyone who wants to crack open the secret to self-leadership, leading others and truly creating a thriving, high performing team, to read and learn from this insightful book. Michelle is a highly credentialed expert who has worked for years helping people and organisations achieve these goals with great results.

Jon Aloni, Activating People for Success

LEADING ABOVE THE LINE

LEADING ABOVE THE LINE:

APPLYING NEUROSCIENCE TO BUILD PSYCHOLOGICALLY SAFE AND THRIVING TEAMS

MICHELLE BIHARY

Edited by Joanna Yardley at The Editing House

Chapter pages designed by Angela Kvasha

Cover design by Jane Radman at Jane Radman Designs

Typeset, printed and bound in Australia by BookPOD

This book uses blended case examples to enforce the meaning behind its relevant chapter. All identifying information has been changed to protect individual and workplace privacy.

Every effort has been made to trace (and seek permission for use of) the original source of material used within this book. Where the attempt has been unsuccessful, the publisher would be pleased to hear from the author / publisher to rectify any omission.

ISBN 978-0-6485696-0-2

NATIONAL LIBRARY OF AUSTRALIA

A catalogue record for this book is available from the National Library of Australia

Contents

Preface

This book is about creating psychologically aware, responsible and safe workplaces that enable people to fulfil their potential and achieve peak performance as they thrive. Never before have the importance of human relationships and the interpersonal climate we collectively create been more critical to our professional lives and to an organisation's success.

In Part One, the reader will learn how workplace challenges result from the psychological environment slipping below what supports humans to function at their best. We call this 'below-the-line' functioning. I will offer insights into research and common experiences that enable us to bring more refined language and perspectives to modern workplace dilemmas. Although some elements in Part One are negative or even depressing, we cannot manage what we're unaware of, nor what we cannot consider, think or talk about.

In Part Two, we'll learn that we must lead ourselves before we can genuinely lead others 'above the line'. Most leaders give scant attention to how they lead themselves, yet it is pivotal to how they lead others.

We'll also explore how leaders can build relationships with each of their employees and address the steps they can take to lead and manage interrelationships within their team and workplace so they (and their team) can rise above the line.

With deep gratitude

'Trust thyself: every heart
vibrates to that iron string.'
—Ralph Waldo Emmerson

This book is dedicated to Mum and Dad who imparted the values of self-trust, listening to one's inner voice and living to the beat of one's own heart and drum.

***

The culmination of years of learning, experience and growth is only possible with the generosity and wisdom of many exceptional people.

It takes a village to birth a book. I deeply honour and acknowledge:

The influential teachings and research of Dr Daniel Siegel, Dr Rick Hanson, Amy Edmondson, Brené Brown, Kristin Neff, Martin Seligman, Bill O'Hanlon, Dr Paul Gibney, Dr Ben Palmer, Stephanie Dowrick, Harriet Lerner, Ken Wilber, Eckhart Tolle, Michael Henderson and his wise teacher (the late) Dr David Hawkins for his contribution to the human consciousness field.

The inspiring mentors who so generously shared their wisdom include Elisabeth Scott, Tom Patterson, Jane Curtis, Lilly Kitchen, Matt Church, Peter Cook, Simon Dowling, Jaquie Scammell, Jane Anderson and the Thought Leaders tribe.

The many inspiring leaders who exemplify the values of this book include: Debbie Gabreal, Jenni Richardson, Faorligh Hunter, Chris Kennedy, Marie Garcia, Cindy Hollings, Kerri Roberts, Anastasia Panayiotidis, Jo Manuell, Joan Leo, Randa Abbasi, Robyn and Tony Stephen, Cynthia Gebert, Sharon Read, Caz Healy, Kath Jones, Brodie Dupre, Catherine Mayhew, and Lauren and McFarlane Pattinson. Along with many thousands of clients and workshop participants who generously shared their stories, challenges and learnings.

My wise colleagues who have become deeply cherished friends: Naomi Kalman—my professional running partner for almost 40 years, Vivienne Moses, Dr Deborah Absler, Kaaren Hawkes, Anastasia Panayiotidis, Olga Varsos, Helen Slucki, Bonita Cohen, Lane Shmerling, Janet Cowling, Diana Coverdale, Harry Gelber OAM, Jacqui Snider, Renee Arnott, and many others including the wonderful Delta Centre team.

My phenomenal dream team including Rita Page, Mary Blazevski, Tamsin Ries, Joel Torbiner and Angela Kvasha for your dedication, contribution and teamwork. Angela, a special mention for your brilliant graphic designs that make my book and work come alive.

I'm deeply grateful to Jo Yardley, my editor and the wind beneath my wings. You elevated my writing and elegantly worked with Sylvie Blair to create this polished book. A special thank you to Jane Radman for a stunning cover design. Tamsin Ries, special recognition for the exceptional and discerning feedback on my writing and your tireless support. The incomparable Kelly Irving, your sage guidance shepherded me from floundering to finding my inner writer, and my dear friend Dr Deborah Absler who generously supported me on my writing journey.

Last, but not least, my treasured family and friends who lovingly enrich my life. My precious sons Yossi and Joel, I couldn't be prouder of you both. I'm deeply grateful for our close relationships and for your support for me personally and for my professional journey. To my partner Pete, for your love, support and dedication to making our home a beautiful sanctuary. To my family, Mum, Judi, Elena, Mary, your precious families and the treasured times we share. To my dear soul sisters, deep gratitude for your haven of love and wisdom.

About Michelle

My lens has always been focused on optimising people's capacity to perform well. I'm an expert in helping leaders build high-performing, psychologically safe and thriving teams. My focus is on amplifying potential, maximising productivity, and optimising workplace relationships and teamwork ensuring wellbeing and resilience remain paramount. I have found using the combined lenses of neuroscience and emotional intelligence, and the interaction between our psychology, relationships and our environment to be most impactful.

In addition to a background in applied science, I have over thirty years' experience as a mental health occupational therapist, psychotherapist and family therapist. Fifteen years ago, I transitioned from focusing on the mental health and wellbeing of people within the community to working with leaders and workplaces to build teams that are high-performing, psychologically safe and resilient.

In particular, I'm sought after to work in organisations where relationships are a critical factor in everyday activities and where emotional 'wear and tear' can be high. These include organisations across Australia and New Zealand and span sectors such as health, mental health, legal, education, justice, police, and complaint handling, and corporations such as IAG, Suncorp, TAC and QBE.

In 2010, I was extremely humbled to receive the National award from my professional association, Occupational Therapy Australia, in recognition of an extensive contribution to my professional field.

Introduction

'It's impossible to build an organisation
that's fit for the future without building
one that's fit for human beings.'
—Gary Hamel

Workplaces give us a front-row seat to the best and worst in humans.

The variations in acceptable workplace behaviour create diverse experiences for employees. This impacts performance, productivity and engagement as well as customer service and workforce wellbeing.

Workplaces differ wildly in the interpersonal environment. I'm sure you can relate to this. What is accepted in some workplaces would be completely out of bounds in others. Even teams within the same organisation can function differently at the interpersonal level.

It is an inconvenient reality that how we behave towards each other at work has an undeniable impact on organisational success.

Over the last 15 years, the opportunity to provide facilitation and training with tens of thousands of professionals in a range of industries has given me unique insights into what is happening in many workplaces and teams.

A potent and sobering part of this experience has been witnessing the impact of a toxic workplace climate and the cost to employees' mental health. The consequences are unbearable.

From insurance companies to health services and banking organisations to legal firms, there is a clear and varied interpersonal environment. Even within one industry, there are tremendous differences in the patterns of behaviour and the psychological climate of the workplace.

Remarkably, some of the least caring workplace environments are those in the business of 'caring' such as health and community services.

Some workplaces are so toxic they have morphed into a battle-to-the-death scene from *Star Wars;* others are as peaceful and harmonious as your local library. Now, libraries may seem mind-numbingly dull, but they are psychologically safe and provide a place to concentrate rather than being caught in the crossfire of a *Star Wars* battle scene.

The extreme variations I witnessed led to many reflections. I have posed them here as questions:

- Are you concerned about the state of contemporary workplaces?
- Are the teams in your vicinity flourishing or floundering?
- How has COVID-19 impacted your workplace climate and how your team functions?
- With the level of uncertainty and complexity COVID-19 presents, how can we support our employees to be ready for the future?

I imagine that your interest or concern about these themes may have encouraged you to pick up this book.

You have probably seen workplaces or teams across the continuum from thriving to struggling or even toxic. Like many leaders, you may have questioned what can be done to shift the dial for a low-performing team. As an employee, you may have questioned whether to stay or leave an unhealthy workplace, particularly where there is a lack of commitment from senior management to address the contributing issues.

In my experience working with many organisations, the following stood out:

- The problems with interpersonal behaviours in workplaces are getting worse.
- The consequences of poor interpersonal actions are wreaking havoc with workplace productivity and performance.
- These issues have a damaging impact on organisational success.
- The effect on the wellbeing of the workforce is destructive and can be traumatising and life-threatening.
- These issues are carried home; they impact our personal lives and our relationships with loved ones.
- These issues contribute to the rise of mental illness in the community.

My interest is in exploring four key questions:

1. Why do workplaces end up at such different places on this continuum?
2. What steps can leaders take to be active stewards of the psychological environment and shift floundering workplaces to healthier functioning?

3. How can we apply the latest neuroscience and emerging psychological research to help elevate and sustain the quality of team relationships?

4. As we emerge from the COVID-19 pandemic, how can we re-imagine and reshape our workplaces to better serve our human needs?

Extensive research highlights that workplace relationships and interpersonal interactions have a profound impact on human performance, productivity, work satisfaction and fulfilment.[1,2,3]

Positive workplace interactions are energising and engaging for humans. They help us feel psychologically safe and they draw out our strengths and values. We can categorise good working relationships as 'above the line'. These working relationships enhance productivity, performance and wellbeing. Negative interactions are below the line. They negatively impact performance, productivity and wellbeing.

When interpersonal relationships are positive and healthy (above the line), they form fertile soil that maximises the capacity of a business or workplace to flourish. Poor relationships and negative interpersonal interactions wreak havoc with the performance and sustainability of any organisation.

Bullying, workplace aggression, incivility, shaming, blaming and disrespectful behaviours are all below the line. Shockingly, and despite the toll they have on the workforce and the success of organisations, their occurrence is increasing.

For those of you who have been working from home during 2020, being away from the intensity of your workplace culture may have provided insights into the quality of your workplace environment. You may have had the space to reflect on your workplace, its strengths and its limitations.

> The workplace environment can either
> support the workforce to flourish or be a
> quagmire of strain, negativity and conflict.

In an environment where pressured KPIs and continually changing demands are prevalent, leaders can struggle to influence workplace culture and interpersonal dynamics. Leaders increasingly recognise that without attention and focus, the psychological climate can quickly spiral below the line.

However, we are still not capitalising on this awareness and utilising the emerging research from neuroscience to harness the best in ourselves and our workplaces.[4]

Although the psychosocial environment is crucial to workplace functioning, it is generally ignored and neglected. Workplaces are usually low on psychological literacy. They lack adequate language to describe and discuss the dynamics at play. Regardless of whether we have the words to explain or even recognise the undercurrents, they are still impactful. Perhaps they are even more powerful when we lack the ability to recognise them and (hence) influence them.

The future frontier for modern leadership is to have a shift in consciousness that builds the sophisticated interpersonal skills necessary to optimise workforce functioning in order to achieve organisational and strategic success. Organisations need to be built on and aligned with the wellbeing of the workforce. Emerging research highlights that organisations are becoming unsustainable when they function at the expense of employees.[5,6,7,8,9,10,11,12]

Right now, moving through the pandemic, we have a once-in-a-lifetime opportunity to shape the workplace of the future. We can use this time to build organisational success founded on peak performance, and the creativity and innovation of the workforce in ways that strongly align with people thriving at work.

I'm confident that you have learned more about yourself, your colleagues and your workplace in recent months. Clarity around the impact of stress, crisis, personal strain and remote working has been difficult. Yet, we have simultaneously been enriched with a deeper level of understanding of ourselves and others and an elevated level of consciousness that can take us to a higher level of functioning.

Many leaders are seeking ways to understand what is going on in the psychological and interpersonal environment; they want to know how to make a difference. If you are such a leader, I hope this book helps you on your journey.

PART ONE

AWARE

Chapter One

WHY LEAD ABOVE
THE LINE?

Impact of the psychological environment

The psychological environment of our contemporary workplace is increasingly harsh and even hostile to optimal human functioning. It undermines an employee's capacity to contribute their best to their organisation's success.

Many current workplace challenges result from poor interpersonal interactions, unrealistic expectations, and a lack of knowledge and understanding of how to create the systemic changes needed to help workplaces thrive. In fact, many workplaces create conditions for their employees that work directly against their stated goals.

A poor interpersonal environment and overwhelming expectations undermine the capacity of employees to function near their capacity and potential.

The complexity of modern workplace demands requires humans to function well cognitively and psychologically. We need to think strategically, laterally and creatively, and make decisions with increasing complexity in the context of uncertainty and diminishing resources.

From a cognitive and psychological perspective, we function well when we have the mental agility and flexibility to see situations from different perspectives including viewpoints with which we may not agree. This high level of functioning happens easily in an interpersonally healthy environment when people feel psychologically and physically safe.

The crisis of COVID-19 has provided leaders with an opportunity for enforced reflection on our workplaces. Many of us have had the chance to deeply consider how to positively influence the psychological health of our team environment, and the creativity and performance of our teams. During this time, we have been more educated about mental health and its critical role in professional performance, and we can see more clearly the impact a poor environment can have on the mental wellbeing of the workforce.

Your organisation and its employees deserve and require the benefits of a psychological environment that enables and ensures humans can perform at their peak. Senior leaders need to safeguard and elevate this environment to achieve organisational success and make their workplace thrive.

Toxic workplaces are all too common

Over every glass of wine, beer or latte, while catching up with family, friends or colleagues, inevitably the conversation will come around to the poor state of someone's workplace.

We know it all too well. Our friend's office is in the middle of a poorly managed organisational restructure; people are facing redundancy and morale has hit rock bottom. Our partner's team is led by a nit-picky micromanager, which results in endless discussions about the impact on their workplace. Or, our cousin works in an organisation hell-bent on ignoring the effect of a senior manager who is a bully, possibly even a psychopath, and is wreaking havoc on the entire department, haemorrhaging their best talent and experiencing unprecedented turnover.

During the pandemic, while many of us are working from home, workplace politics have shapeshifted into different forms. Bullies are finding ways to use social media to continue their harassment and others are exploiting the isolation of their direct reports to inconspicuously wreak psychological warfare.

Unfortunately, the above scenarios are not isolated incidents. They are examples of what we expect to be an almost inevitable part of the contemporary workplace. Employees head into the office (physically or remotely) each day gearing up for the unpredictable onslaught of interpersonal pressures and unmanaged egos. Many workplaces ignore the impact this has on their employees' capacity to perform their roles and the strain it creates professionally and personally for a committed workforce. Despite the stream of defectors from corporations to start-up nirvana, emerging research shows that the interpersonal issues and pressures may be no better managed in this newer frontier.[13,14,15]

Overwhelming pressures are counterproductive

Leaders and employees everywhere are overwhelmed. According to Deloitte and many other researchers, global trends show that over the past decade, the modern workforce is experiencing a cascading set of unprecedented stressors and demands.[16,17]

Most leaders and employees I speak with are mentally and emotionally exhausted from facing excessive cognitive and psychological demands. They have way more work than is possible to complete within their working hours and they often experience unrealistic pressures and challenges.

The most troubling aspects have been the significant interpersonal tensions and conflict, and the irresponsible, hostile and aggressive behaviours that are increasingly commonplace in our workplaces. Coupled with the constant requirement to adapt and change, these challenges create immense strain. Far from helping us perform at our peak, these pressures promote reactivity and undermine our ability to bring our best to the workplace. They also encourage us to slip into patterns of behaviour that we would consider below the line: actions that are distressing to be on the receiving end of and that create significant stress, mental health issues and even trauma.

Humans are wired for self-protection

In an environment that is psychologically unsafe, humans instinctively shift into self-protection mode. If we sense that a colleague is in a bad mood, or is irritable or unreliable, we are more likely to be on guard. This is amplified when a manager or group of colleagues operates in less predictable, impatient or overly critical ways.

We all have a primitive part of our brain that is programmed to scan our environment continually to ensure we are physically and psychologically safe. It's like our antivirus software. If the primitive or reptilian part of our brain detects a threat to our physical or psychological safety, our brain redirects its attention to survival and self-protection. This antivirus software then takes precedence, using most of our human processing power to deal with the risk at hand.

If we are working in an environment where one has to exert significant mental and emotional energy in self-protection, it takes a substantial cognitive and emotional load to keep concentrating on one's work demands simultaneously. The superhuman effort that this requires creates enormous drain and strain.

I hear many leaders and employees describe feeling unsafe at work, mostly psychologically unsafe. Perhaps stormtrooper gear would be more appropriate attire for the toxic or harmful environment in which they find themselves.

Well-meaning guidance to cope with contemporary workplace demands can further complicate the situation. Suggesting a mindfulness app, lunchtime yoga class or employee assistance session by way of enduring a psychologically toxic environment is unreasonable and potentially damaging. It unfairly places the responsibility for dealing with the stressors on the employee.

The impossible challenge of work / life balance

Added to this are the changes in how we are working. No longer are there clear distinctions between work and home. The boundaries are blurred; employees are increasingly expected to be available for extended work hours or out of work hours' contact. This further exacerbates the problem where the cognitive and psychological demands of work drain the bulk of each employee's energy reserves. This has been amplified during the pandemic period.

Often, employees describe how they end each workday absolutely gutted, with nothing left for themselves or their loved ones. No-one wants to live and work like this. The pandemic has amplified the need to refocus on our highest priorities and life goals.

The demands of the contemporary
workplace require that we often borrow
from home, in order to pay for work.

Is this sustainable both for humans and organisations?

Leaders and employees everywhere are asking whether this way of working is sustainable for the success of the workplace and the workforce. Many organisations are haemorrhaging talent. This will increase if they do not adjust their business models. COVID-19 has opened people's eyes to the alternatives. Organisations are losing access to their employees' potential and capabilities. Levels of absenteeism, presenteeism, disengagement and burnout are unacceptably high and rising exponentially. High turnover in some industries makes it difficult to provide consistent customer service, which alienates a loyal customer base. Emerging research shows that factors such as turnover and absenteeism are impacting customer service in many areas, ultimately placing the workforce under increased pressure.[18,19,20] In healthcare, for example, these factors put the community at higher risk.

Leaders are looking for ways to create human sustainability. As well as recognising the serious impact on business priorities, we can no longer ignore the human cost, and the moral and ethical dilemmas of unacceptable workplace pressures.

The current pandemic has repositioned and elevated the importance of mental health and wellbeing. The government and media have never more clearly addressed the vital role that mental health plays in our community. One of the most common questions I have been asked this year by leaders managing employees remotely is how to check in and ensure their colleagues are travelling OK.

In 2019, the World Health Organization (WHO) took the unprecedented step of classifying 'burnout syndrome' as an occupational phenomenon. This move highlights that burnout is not a medical condition and should not be used to describe experiences in other areas of life.

The WHO outlined three key characteristics of burnout:

1. Feelings of energy depletion and exhaustion.
2. Increased mental distance from one's job, and feelings of negativism and cynicism.
3. Reduced professional effectiveness.

Humans, not robots

The modern-day workplace has not adequately taken into account how humans are wired. This level of denial of our human selves is a key factor in why we are experiencing an explosion of burnout, overwhelm and workplace stress. Workplaces do not adequately consider how we function from a biological, neuroscientific, psychological or interpersonal perspective. In fact, the approach of some workplaces is to treat its employees like automatons—they are expected to work like robots. (Some examples include legal work and call centres.) Perhaps it's not surprising that stormtrooper suits might feel more protective.

To ensure employees have the best chance of applying their greatest skills and capacities in their professional roles, we need to understand, actively shape and manage the environment that supports them to function at their peak.

But we pay them very well

Some organisations reassure themselves that a strong salary package compensates for workplace pressures. However, the belief that a truckload of money will circumvent the professional and personal impact is gravely mistaken. No amount of money, status or perks can put a stop to the long-term damage that some of the worst dynamics and pressures create. In his book, *Dying for a Paycheck*, Jeffrey Pfeffer challenges the current thinking about work and brings together immense research to show that employees across the globe are dying from overwork. Some dying literally, and some dying from the absence of meaning because work is sucking every ounce of their mental and emotional energy.[21]

Some of us are witness or subject to the worst of what the world of work has to offer: workplace bullying, harassment or discrimination. These behaviours take many forms: incivility, shaming, unacceptable expressions of anger, overt or covert hostility, aggression, contempt and antagonism, blaming, unpredictability, frequent criticism, negating, sarcasm, eye-rolling, social isolation … the list goes on.

These behaviours are all below the line. They have a negative psychological impact. Especially when sustained, they damage our mental health and wellbeing, and cause mental health issues and trauma.

At the most devastating end, they have unbearably heartbreaking consequences. Research shows that workplace stressors and bullying result in increased suicide rates, mental illness, trauma and serious physical illness to name a few.[22,23,24]

Questions for reflection:

What is happening in your world?

What are you observing in your workplace?

How does your current work environment compare with others in which you have worked?

How would you describe the interpersonal environment?

Rethinking work

Look at what's happening in our world. We are seeing complex advances in technology and how we are living our lives. We are experiencing a time where people are burning out from working 12–15-hour days. The way we are working is not sustainable. We're expecting more with less.

We're all seeking simple solutions to that complexity.

Meanwhile, there are countries like Sweden that have explored working six-hour days. There are innovative companies that have found a four-day working week has led to higher productivity, more motivated employees and less burnout. These organisations are living in alignment with extensive research, which highlights that we perform at our peak when we work less than 40 hours per week.[25,26,27,28,29,30] We are not achieving more by working more hours. Instead, we take 45 or 55 hours to complete the same amount of work, and we suffer because we have significantly fewer hours to replenish and recharge.

The unhealthy workplace

We need to rethink the cost of work on our health and wellbeing. Never have we been so aware of the negative impact that our stressful and sedentary life is having. We sit for many hours a day glued to technology; we are disconnected from the environment, nature and sunlight, and distanced from the most critical relationships in our lives including our relationship with ourselves.

Research shows that what we are doing workwise is not sustainable.[31,32] We need to think structurally, strategically and systemically about how we can work differently. Part of this inquiry must consider how to boost productivity so we can perform at our peak while being mindful that we maintain wellbeing and a meaningful home life.

iRobot no more

We can't solve 21st-century challenges with 20th- or mid-20th-century solutions.

Schools often teach us to be a cog in the production line. However, accelerating advances in technology, societal changes, social media and robotic social engineering (for want of a better word) is falling away. Today, there's greater freedom to be truer to ourselves and our individuality, and in how we live and the life choices we make. The explosion in microbusinesses, entrepreneurships and online companies are examples of this.

Solutions that revert to old-fashioned thinking are dying out. Today, we know ourselves in a way that brings out the finest within us. In our yoga-centric, mindful and self-development environment, we value living with authenticity and integrity, bringing out our potential and utilising autonomy to take responsibility for ourselves. And research supports this.[33] Being authentic, being open about learning, and living and working in alignment with our values is good for us and far better for our workplaces.

Are organisations lacking self-awareness?

At an organisational level, businesses are losing credibility with a public that demands trust and social responsibility. Increasingly, boards are under pressure to address the deficit in public trust that has given social-media savvy consumers defining power not previously available. The community is disillusioned by organisations that have shirked their responsibilities to care for their customers and employees. Businesses are increasingly under pressure to act with integrity and decency, and to ensure their shareholders are no longer the only beneficiaries—everyone must profit from their endeavours.

> Stress is the chronic disease of the workplace and bullying is the malignant cancer.

Some workplaces have developed a total disregard for human and personal consequences of unreasonable workplace expectations or treatment. In these workplaces, when people are underperforming, are unproductive or are not meeting KPIs, the responsibility and blame is placed on the employee. They are performance-managed, dressed down, humiliated or shamed. There is no consideration of the degree to which the toxic environment has played a role. If someone raises this as a possibility, the idea is shut down and all the responsibility is placed back on the employee.

'When a flower doesn't bloom,
you fix the environment in which
it grows, not the flower.'
—Alexander den Heijer

Is resilience the key?

When an employee is overwhelmed, or unable to cope with overwork and impossible demands, we frequently blame the individual. We infer they are not resilient. These words can be heard in the most alarming places like hospitals and emergency departments, where doctors and staff are expected to work superhuman hours and carry impossibly high caseloads beyond what is physically (or emotionally) possible.

Recent Australian research into bullying and the psychosocial safety climate highlights that as an employee's psychological and emotional workload increases, so does the prevalence of bullying.[34,35] More 'caring' environments like healthcare and community services can be the least caring for their workforce.

It is shocking to know that at least five large Australian public health services have lost their medical training accreditations in the last few years because of workplace bullying.[36,37,38,39] Even more heartbreaking is the increasing level of suicide rates among doctors and nurses. This situation is outrageous in workplaces that have the expertise to comprehend fully and act on the physical and psychological consequences of such demands.

We recognise resilience as a vital skill in today's workplace. Undoubtedly, many people can benefit from building skills in adaptability. However, it seems we are misusing this concept. We now expect employees to use resilience to cope with inhumane working hours or to tolerate toxic workplace behaviour or culture. No amount of resilience training can help the human mind, body or soul cope with unreasonable demands or a highly toxic interpersonal environment.

Basic needs to thrive

For people to thrive, to perform at their peak, and to be engaged and motivated, their core human needs must be met. It has been well established by writers such as Maslow and Hanson that we all share common human needs.[40,41] It has become vital for organisations to take heed of this understanding and to not expect employees to work long hours that result in them having little energy to take home to fulfil their human needs.

What are our common and essential human needs?

1. **Safety:** both physical and psychological.
2. The need to feel **Valued**: that we are worthy and we matter.
3. **Fulfilment**: to have meaning and purpose, to develop ourselves, to have opportunities to learn, grow and develop and to benefit from meaningful activities and from fun and satisfaction.
4. **Connection**: positive relationships at home *and* at work.

In the context of overwhelming demands, when work requires the bulk of our physical, mental and emotional energy, it is easy to see how hard it is to fulfil these needs adequately. Emerging research points to this as one contributor to the escalating rates of depression.[42]

Mental health research

Research into the mental health of the workforce reveals that when our core human needs are not being met, we are highly vulnerable to an increased risk of mental illness. It highlights that when employees feel unsafe, unfulfilled and disconnected they are 200–300 per cent more likely to experience mental illnesses such as depression or anxiety.[43,44,45]

- Employees feel unsafe when they are subject to excessively high work demands. They feel psychologically and / or physically unsafe.
- Employees feel unfulfilled when they have little control or influence over their work—there is a lack of fulfilment.
- Employees feel disconnected when they are socially isolated at work, or when they don't feel valued or when they feel they don't matter.

In contrast, research shows that when C-suite and senior management increases commitment to promoting psychological health and safety, the prevalence of workplace bullying decreases.[46,47]

The old way was organisational success at the expense of the workforce. The new way is organisational success aligned with employees' potential, productivity and wellbeing.

Thriving ecosystem from the top

The purpose of this book is to enable people to fulfil their potential, and to help create peak performance and thriving workplaces. It is about what happens when senior leaders require that the organisation aligns with above-the-line behaviours that genuinely prioritise people and their wellbeing so that they can truly perform at their peak.

To achieve a thriving workplace, senior leaders must create an ecosystem that supports people to perform at their peak while sustaining resilience and wellbeing. This can only happen when the workplace prioritises the productivity, potential and wellbeing of the workforce at all levels of organisational functioning. This 'whole systems' approach involves leadership and management approaches, workplace culture and the psychological safety of the workplace.

A thriving ecosystem helps capture the notion that all elements interlink and influence each other. It harnesses and amplifies the positive aspects of workplace functioning that lead to a thriving organisation. It is not that the business or workplace thrives at the expense of other parts; it is that the 'whole' thrives in a way that calibrates with everyone thriving. If COVID-19 has taught us anything, it's who is needed and the value they bring.

Your company needs all of you

The nature of the modern workplace requires so much more of our engagement and individuality. Think about service industries where it's no longer adequate to be a widget in a factory. Today, we expect employees to bring their whole selves to work; personality, energy, sense of humour, relationship skills and the willingness to work as part of the team are all highly valued and essential workplace skills.

We're not paid to show up physically and work like a robot. Showing up with just our knowledge and intellect is not enough. Customer service expectations require that we bring our heart and soul to work. It's about relationships, teamwork, connection and belonging. It's about engaging (with customers or with colleagues) and the impact that has on our workplace and workforce. It's about who we are as people physically, mentally and emotionally at a deeper soul level.

We call these traits 'soft skills', yet these are the hardest skills to learn and teach.

When workplaces measure employee engagement, they are measuring the degree to which their people bring their whole selves to work. Are they just turning up and being compliant and sleepwalking through their day, or are they engaged, passionate, caring and contributing to the team and the workplace?

For employees to bring their whole selves to work, they need to feel valued and appreciated, not like a commodity that can be readily replaced. The contract is two-way: when workplaces value employees as whole humans, employees will bring their whole selves to the workplace.

IN SUMMARY

In this chapter, we've examined how workplaces vary in how the psychological environment functions and how it is managed by senior leaders. We've noticed that workplaces can function above or below the line, and that above the line is good for workplace success and is vital in supporting thriving and resilient employees.

In the next chapter, we explore how the workplace functions as a psychological environment, where 'the line' is and how it can be influenced.

Questions for reflection:

What words would capture your best days and worst days at work?

Do you see it getting better, staying constant or getting worse?

Regardless of whether you have a positive or negative experience, what factors do you believe contribute to this?

What are the worst behaviours you observe in your workplace?

How does your workplace deal with this at the time?

How does your workplace deal with this in the long term?

What about your close family and friends? Reflect on how they might answer these questions?

Chapter Two

EVERYONE NEEDS
ABOVE-THE-LINE
LEADERSHIP

Christina Maslach, an expert on workplace burnout and vicarious traumatisation, says, 'If you have people who have burnout, it is the canary in the coal mine showing that your workplace is toxic. The answer can't just be [to] make the canary more resilient, the answer is to treat the toxic workplace'.[48]

Meet Team Acacia

About two years ago, I met a team (I'll call it Team Acacia) who worked with severely mentally unwell illicit drug users in the local community. The work carried significant risks as the reluctant clients were court ordered to engage in treatment.

Although the professionals were highly dedicated to serving this complex and troubled client group, the interpersonal dynamics of the team had become increasingly dysfunctional—even toxic. Staff turnover was high, and the leaders were struggling to recruit due to their poor reputation.

As trust within the team deteriorated, staff resorted to the risky practice of doing solo home visits to clients living in extremely rough environments. For the leaders, this shift was the trigger for seeking external support.

When I met with the senior leadership team, the tension and lack of teamwork were palpable. Team members spoke over each other, and eye-rolling and other mocking behaviours were common. I heard about the everyday interactions of the team members and how much of it had slipped below the line. When they described team interactions, there was bitching, gossiping, excluding, negating and judgemental criticism. With such a high level of positive commitment to their clients, it was a little shocking to witness the stark contrast in their attitudes and relationships with each other. This team, who was so highly empathic towards very complex clients, lacked any compassion and kindness for one another.

As team members spoke, I came to the disturbing realisation that they felt greater trust and psychological safety with their high-risk clients than with each other. This was a dangerous place for them to be. It was a clear indicator of how toxic things had become.

***

As I take stock of what was occurring in this team's work environment, I'm sure you're also thinking:

- How does a team's level of goodwill deteriorate so dramatically?
- How do workplaces deal with these issues?
- What can assist a team to shift upwards from toxic to peak performance?

Luckily, not every team strays so far below the line. Yet, Team Acacia illustrates how a highly committed and professional team can spiral downwards despite its best intentions. Not only is it vital to get above the line, it is essential to understand how to make this sustainable.

Many organisations are genuinely working to elevate the psychological climate by recognising their legislative responsibility to create psychologically safe and mentally healthy workplaces. However, research is still developing a clearer understanding of what specific factors create and perpetuate below-the-line functioning as well as how to elevate and sustain an enhanced climate.

Pitfalls of current solutions

Our current responses to poorly functioning workplaces and teams do not always shift things adequately. Often, they are not systemic and holistic.

- They are reactive.
- They are piecemeal.
- They (often) seek someone to blame.
- They address issues individually.
- They are divisive. For example, they highlight differences, not similarities using personality inventories.
- They are focused on gathering data such as engagement statistics but then don't know what to do with the numbers.
- Leaders spend a lot of time fighting fires rather than leading.
- HR is too busy troubleshooting; it becomes constrained from more systemic and structural solutions.
- They are not integrated, modelled or endorsed from the top of the organisation.

Can you see this happening in your workplace?

The truth of it is tragic. Most people come to work to participate constructively and positively and are tired of these matters not being adequately addressed. To tackle these issues more directly, we need to deepen our understanding of the workplace as an interpersonal environment.

What is the psychological and interpersonal environment?

We must recognise that the workplace is a psychological and interpersonal environment.

Just because the psychological environment is invisible doesn't mean it is not highly potent, either positively or negatively.

The psychological and interpersonal environment is (part of) what we refer to as workplace culture. However, by combining it with all the other elements of culture, we can ignore or avoid the specifics of the psychological and interpersonal dynamics, patterns and interactions.

It is the sum of all the psychological and interpersonal dynamics and interactions of every member of the workplace. These dynamics are fluid and flowing; they are influenced by behaviours and attitudes and by people's vibe or energy.

All relationships have **psychological contracts**. The psychological contract is the implicit and unspoken agreement about what behaviours are acceptable and what behaviours are unacceptable in each workplace. The psychological contract is established through everyday interactions and the concept was articulated as early as the 1960s by Chris Argyris in his book, *Understanding Organizational Behavior*.[49]

The psychological contract is fluid and will be formed and shaped by daily interactions. In the case of Team Acacia, these interactions slowly spiralled into a vicious cycle that was difficult to end.

In any workplace, the senior leadership team sets the tone of the psychological contract. This will happen regardless of how aware the team is of these dynamics and its impact on them.

To optimise the psychological and interpersonal environment of the workplace, we need to actively become aware of it, learn to read it, tune in to it, and develop language and concepts to understand and describe what is occurring.

Can we influence what we can't see?

If the psychological landscape and contract are as highly influential as we have come to understand, how do we manage that in a workplace environment?

Do we need every leader to have a psychology degree?

How is it possible to influence the workplace environment without this?

We need to understand some basics about how humans function, and how this impacts the workforce, its performance and its wellbeing. We invest far more into our IT infrastructure than the psychological infrastructure we also rely on to fulfil our organisation's business goals.

To optimise workplace performance, potential and wellbeing, we need to actively prioritise and positively influence the psychological and interpersonal environment.

Once we recognise that the psychological environment can be influenced, we can see more clearly how this impacts progress for individuals, teams and the organisation as a whole.

Leaders are in positions to influence the psychological and interpersonal environment. Within Team Acacia, leaders set the tone for how people related to each other. Through using their influence as role models, leaders can be psychologically responsible for building a thriving environment *or* creating a fear-driven, unsafe environment. As the old saying goes, 'A fish rots from the head'. Therefore, leaders need to set the tone far above the line.

> *'The culture of any organization is shaped by the worst behaviour the leader is willing to tolerate.'*
> —Gruenert and Whitaker

Every employee and organisation needs the benefit of above-the-line leadership. Leading an organisation above the line assists with many of the intractable issues that workplaces struggle to address as outlined in Chapter One.

Questions for reflection:

Is your team above or below the line?

How far is your team above or below the line?

I'm hoping your team has not dipped below the line. Maybe you're still not sure of what or where the line is, so let's explore that.

Where is the line?

Let's examine the concept of above the line and below the line.

If above the line and below the line are significant, the questions we have to consider are: Where is the line? And, if we cannot see the line, is it even that important?

Having recognised that we operate in a psychological and interpersonal landscape, we can see that sometimes this is healthy, responsible and generative but at other times is less healthy.

> The 'line' separates what is healthy, safe
> and responsible, and what is unacceptable,
> unhealthy, unsafe and irresponsible.

The point between healthy (what's good for people, teams and work environments) and unhealthy (what's bad and unhelpful to people, teams and work environments) determines the location of the line.

The line itself represents a band of behaviours that are more transactional in nature—behaviours that are neither positively nor negatively impactful. When you walk into a store and purchase something with minimal interaction with the employee, it is a fairly neutral transaction—it is 'on the line'.

However, if you share a laugh, show genuine interest in the salesperson and you both leave the interaction feeling a little brighter, this is above the line. If you criticise the salesperson and behave contemptuously, this is a below-the-line interaction. The line must be where the environment is neutral and has no impact on positive or negative functioning.

Everyone has the fundamental human right to be safe at work (and in any other environment like at home or within the community). For many years, Australian workplaces have been legislated to provide a physically safe work environment. More recently, this has been extended to ensure a psychologically safe environment.

Above the line

Behaviours and actions are acceptable, healthy and responsible from a human, psychological and interpersonal perspective. These behaviours and actions form, shape and create workplaces that are in the best interests of people (individuals or teams). There is a solid psychological basis, which means the organisation works to bring out the best in people, helping them to function at their peak and enabling their best capacities cognitively, creatively and psychologically.

Below the line

Behaviours and actions are not acceptable, healthy or responsible from a psychological and human perspective. They are not in the best interests of people in the workforce, whether it be one person, a group or the workforce in its entirety.

What influences where the line is set?

The line delineates between what is healthy and unhealthy, and reflects what is best for our collective future.

Above the line

When the psychological landscape is above the line and aligned with what is good for people, it inevitably brings out their best. This turbocharges organisational goals and amplifies the potential of the workplace.

The complexity of the modern workplace requires humans to function well cognitively and psychologically. We need to think strategically, laterally and creatively, and make decisions with increasing complexity. And we need to do this within the context of much uncertainty.

From a psychological perspective, we function best in decision-making and strategic planning when we have the psychological agility and flexibility to see situations from different angles, including perspectives with which we may not agree. This high level of cognitive and psychological functioning only happens in a healthy environment when people feel safe psychologically and physically.

Below the line

It does not serve your future or your organisation's success for people to feel unsafe at work. When we're in a continual state of survival, and feel gutted and exhausted from the psychological and cognitive drain, we have no capacity to prepare for the future let alone bring our best capacities to today's challenges. Such antivirus software makes our best thinking and functioning unavailable.

When workplace relationships are operating below the line, it is not a psychologically safe environment. This has a significant impact on how we function. When teams are operating below the line, they lose cognitive and psychological flexibility; they make poorer decisions and are much less strategic. If their work demands high-level cognitive, interpersonal or psychological functioning, it is far more mentally exhausting to keep working in a below-the-line environment.

What leads a team below the line?

When under significant stress or pressure, we can all revert to below-the-line behaviours. I imagine most of us have observed this in ourselves and others during this pandemic. When we're stressed, how easy is it to externalise it and to be narky, grumpy, rude or dismissive with others? If such poor behaviours are not addressed, they can lead the team or workplace to spiral below the line.

When we are not feeling safe, our 'reptile brain' is more activated, and we function in more reactive and less considered ways. When our reptile brain is active, it is much harder for us to access our 'executive brain' (in particular, the middle section or part of the prefrontal cortex)[50], which is the source of our best thinking and psychological functioning.

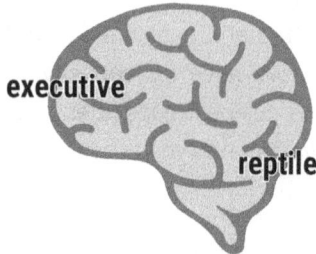

Below-the-line environments feed the reptile brain of the workforce, hampering people's ability to access their skills and best intentions for their performance and productivity.

Override the reptile brain

We can all tolerate some degree of negative interaction but that needs to be well managed. Too often I hear negative managers say their employees are 'not resilient enough'. This is when they expect their employees to remain unaffected by below-the-line behaviour. However, this is asking the humanly impossible. It is not possible to override our reptile brain and not be activated by behaviour and interactions that generate fear. When we operate from the reptile brain, we are fearful, aggressive or competitive, and we play out automatic patterns of behaviour. This, generally, does not serve us or the situation well.

Many current workplace challenges result from interpersonal interactions and expectations undermining the peak brain functioning of employees. This leads people to function from their reptile brain.

When the interpersonal interactions and expectations dip below the line, leaders can feel stuck and overwhelmed. This can negatively impact performance and productivity, interpersonal relationships, teamwork, engagement and bottom-line success.

The solutions to these stresses differ depending on the workplace culture.

Can one person's toxic behaviour bring a team below the line?

Unfortunately, the behaviour of a bully, psychopath or narcissist can be impactful on a whole team. One person's bad behaviour is not counterbalanced by another person's good behaviour. An ecosystem requires many healthy parts to deal with one unhealthy part. We need to address the toxic impact of psychopaths and narcissists who can bring a team to its knees if not managed adequately.

Research by Stephen Dimmock and William C. Gerken shows that misconduct has a social multiplier.[51] The impact of one or two employees who behave badly is significant and can infect an otherwise healthy workplace. Outbreaks of misconduct become viral. We learn and imitate our social norms from each other. When a couple of people start being bitchy or gossiping, it can lead to others joining in, and soon, many team members may let their standards go and continue with below-the-line behaviours.

(Refer to the section *Terminally below the line* in Chapter Five.)

Who determines where the line is?

This is an excellent point for discussion and debate. The most straightforward answer may be to reflect on research that tells us which environments, workplace cultures and relationships support people to function at their best.

Emerging evidence from neuroscience, psychology and specialised areas such as interpersonal neurobiology provides immense detail about the importance of psychological safety, respect and trust, and the impact that the psychological environment has on cognitive and psychological functioning. The research shows that when a person feels safe, the positive impact is felt through their nervous system through chemicals like serotonin, dopamine and oxytocin. Additionally, neural pathways optimise cognitive and psychological skills and relax the entire nervous system.[52,53,54,55]

Recognising that some workplace environments were good for people and others were not, I began to summarise consistent patterns. The following table evolved from my observations.

	PSYCHOLOGICAL ENVIRONMENT	IMPACT ON ORGANISATIONAL SUCCESS	PEOPLE FUNCTION	RISKS TO THE ORGANISATION AND EMPLOYEES
5	PEAK	HIGH	AT THEIR BEST	VERY LOW
4	PRODUCTIVE	MODERATE	WELL	LOW
3	SURVIVAL	BARELY SATISFACTORY	ADEQUATELY	SIGNIFICANT
2	NEGATIVE	NEGATIVE	POORLY	HIGH
1	TOXIC	DAMAGING	DYSFUNCTIONALLY	VERY HIGH

ABOVE THE LINE (5, 4)

BELOW THE LINE (3, 2, 1)

Let's examine each level of functioning of the psychological environment and the impact each has on organisational success and employees.

Toxic

What impact does a toxic workplace have on organisational success and employee functioning?

A toxic workplace actively undermines the ability of the workforce to use its current skills and capacities, let alone develop and innovate individually or collectively.

A toxic workplace is riddled with damaging, poor interpersonal behaviours. When we think about toxic behaviours, we think about bullying, harassment and discrimination. However, there are many more behaviours that are highly toxic and undermine the interpersonal fabric of the workplace. Behaviours that are overtly or covertly hostile, contemptuous, shaming, excluding, gaslighting, aggressive, micromanaging and arrogant are highly damaging to teamwork, trust and the mental wellbeing of the workforce.

One of my earliest bosses (head of the workplace) loved to shame and deride his staff. He always wore a bow tie and you knew that when he fiddled excessively with it, he was preparing to attack. Everyone avoided speaking in his presence through fear of being humiliated. Employees did their best to hide and avoid participating in meetings; it was so inhibitory to teamwork and quality services.

When the psychological environment is toxic, your employees' capacity to use the skills for which you hired them will be compromised. A toxic environment will take the best parts of their brain 'offline'; their wellbeing will be compromised; and their ability to productively contribute to the bottom line and future of your organisation will be severely hampered. In this scenario, employees are more likely to see things 'only' from their perspective.

Team Acacia is an example of a toxic workplace, where the reptile brains of its employees were on full alert. This resulted in them functioning from fear, and in automatic and unconscious patterns. They operated from a 'me-against-you' mindset and lost their cognitive and psychological agility, which reinforced reactivity.

The consequences

A toxic workplace results in lower productivity as we have less access to our best thinking and reasoning skills. All the research on psychological safety from Amy Edmondson and Project Aristotle at Google reinforces how vital feeling safe is to productive teamwork.[56,57,58]

Toxic workplaces create fertile ground for primitive aspects of human behaviour to take hold; therefore, bullying, incivility, and blame and shame dynamics are more likely to dominate. WorkCover stress claims are escalating exponentially and psychological injury is a significant contributing factor. As described in Chapter One, workplace incivility and bullying is reaching epidemic proportions in Australia.

Unacceptable behaviour puts the workplace under high levels of risk at all levels. It affects standards of work, teamwork and the capacity of people to function at their best cognitively and psychologically. Employees are more likely to be combative, easily triggered and overreactive. This contributes to escalating cycles of negativity, toxicity and conflict that damage the psychological and interpersonal environment, and the psychological safety of the workplace. This is a breeding ground for high employee turnover and an unstable workforce environment.

Workforce wellbeing is undermined in a toxic environment and leads to mental and emotional exhaustion. It is hard to continue to cognitively and psychologically perform well when the environment is continually triggering the human brain to be fearful.

It is no wonder so much of the workforce return home gutted each day, having little energy left for themselves and their loved ones.

Negative

What impact does a negative workplace have on organisational success and employee functioning?

A workplace that is functioning at a negative level hampers its success by overly focusing on the negative. This hinders its employees' capacity to perform and thrive. Although this type of environment is not as caustic as a toxic one, it is far from healthy or helpful.

An organisation with a predominantly negative psychological environment has dropped below the line and shifted to overly focusing on negatives, weaknesses and mistakes. What arises is judgement, and negative and critical perceptions. We'd be likely to observe critical and harsh feedback, gossip, bitchiness, contempt, blaming and defensiveness.

I recently worked with a business that fell into this category. The organisation was so focused on meeting KPIs and performance in a negative way that its employees were never given positive feedback. The main focus of their feedback was on what they were doing wrong and how their work was not good enough. The intention of their managers was positive—they wanted to build productivity and output. Unfortunately, the way they went about it was disempowering and de-energising, and it worked against achieving their aim.

A negative environment creates grey-coloured glasses where we see things from 'lack' and a negative lens. Research in positive psychology shows that the lens we apply filters out much available information, just like grey-coloured glasses would filter out the richness and vibrancy of the colours of a rainbow.[59]

With a negative lens, we are more likely to notice and amplify the negatives and ignore the positives. This is not woo-woo; it is cutting-edge science. When humans become habituated to notice the negatives, they see them in more detail. The part of their brain that looks for the negatives becomes more developed and attuned. It's a little like what happens when we are looking to buy a red car. Suddenly, all we notice on the road are red cars.

If our negative lens becomes our habituated way of viewing the world, we can fixate on negatives and problems, and see them as situations to be fixed and solved. We see them as execution problems where someone is doing the right thing or the wrong thing rather than seeing them as opportunities for learning. Humans have a tendency to overlook the positives, especially skills and strengths. This imbalance often results in overlooking opportunities to develop our people and build skills. We become more focused on 'fixing' people.

The consequences

Negative workplaces may have less bullying and incivility than toxic workplaces but are still a long way from bringing out the best in their employees. These workplaces lack trust, cohesion and a shared vision. Interpersonal relationships do not feel safe or consistent; instead, they are critical.

The behaviours that will undermine the potential for quality teamwork include defensiveness, unreliability, incivility, gossiping, bitchiness, impatience, mean-spiritedness, inflexibility and pettiness. These behaviours may reflect a lack of cohesion and goodwill. Negative teams will struggle with adapting to change; they will be less resilient and more vulnerable in riskier states. They will be reactive and avoidant.

The capacity to be innovative and agile to the ever-changing demands of the organisation will be severely compromised. As there is little focus on strengths and development, employees and their teams will struggle to perform well.

A negative environment is not a safe space to learn, grow and develop. Workplace challenges are seen as execution problems. Employees who don't perform in their role as expected are assumed to be ill-disciplined or incompetent. This sidelines a commitment to workplace learning and brings a more punitive and critical approach to underperformance.

Survival

What impact does a survival mode workplace have on organisational success and employee functioning?

Teams in survival mode are starved of energy, resources and positivity.

When functioning in survival mode, organisations do not bring out the best in their people or maximise potential. Like a drought-impacted garden, these workplaces flounder from a lack of positive energy (not so much from negativity or toxicity). These workplaces are going through the motions, just getting by, not flourishing and not engaging.

As with a 'negative' team, the theme of the survival workplace is 'lack'. The behaviours we would most likely observe are lack of motivation, resilience, flexibility, consistency, ownership and cooperation, and a focus on compliance rather than positive engagement.

The consequences

As this level of functioning provides an 'ordinary' but not engaging work experience, it fails to keep top-talent employees who are seeking opportunities to flourish in their professional roles. Innovation and creativity are rare. Employees are likely to be tired, weary and drained of energy as the workplace environment is not supportive or energising.

The survival workplace is compliant; things are done by the book with little energy or engagement. This workplace ticks the boxes but is not actively aligned to the vision and strategic plan of the organisation. The way the workplace functions is unlikely to be an adequate expression of its organisational values. What is missing in survival organisations is the trust necessary to examine and debate different perspectives.

Productive

What impact does a productive workplace have on organisational success and employee functioning?

A productive workplace is a quantum leap from previous styles of functioning.

Positive workplaces are more agile and make a valuable contribution to those they serve—their employees and the community. Employees have adequate self-management skills and team goodwill to rise above the challenges and negativity that difficult work may bring.

Employees of these teams are positive contributors to the workplace culture, freeing their leaders up to focus on driving towards organisational success rather than being bogged down in fighting fires. People need a conducive environment to maintain their performance and productivity. This is only sustainable if it fosters a supportive environment in all interpersonal interactions, not just those expected with customers or clients.

The benefits

There are benefits of a productive workplace for every stakeholder, leader and employee, as well as for business endeavours, productivity, performance and wellbeing.

The energy of the workforce is freed up to drive the business goals and aims, which results in organisational success, employee fulfilment and engagement. When employees are not bogged down with fighting against toxic or negative interpersonal interactions, their capacity for complex thinking, decision-making and collaboration advances innovation and creativity.

Peak

What impact does a peak performance workplace have on organisational success and employee functioning?

Peak performance teams maximise business outcomes, and employee potential and wellbeing.

A peak performance workplace is a thriving ecosystem where people are collaborative and engaged. They fulfil their potential and feel psychologically safe enough to take informed risks and be open to learning and feedback.

Workplaces like this are a rich and valuable resource, and they understand the value of investing in building a positive psychological landscape. In this environment, the skills of self-leadership and self-management are valued; it is safe for employees to be self-aware.

The ability to maintain a high level of performance is not just an individual responsibility. It is profoundly influenced by the ecosystem the employees work within. The approach and support of leaders and the psychological safety of the workplace culture are significant determinants of employees' performance. The safer one feels, the easier it is to stay centred and offer the best innovative thinking and customer service experience.

The benefits

A peak performance workforce produces excellent customer service and values ambassadors who personify the principles the organisation strives to achieve.

Employees bring their discretionary energy to work in ways that advance the organisation through innovation and excellence.

The level of psychological safety, collaboration and positivity in the work environment ensures that highly engaged employees can stay calm in a storm. The robust workplace maintains the positive energy and engagement of the workforce even when dealing with unexpected, unpredictable, challenging and complex situations.

Leaders as guardians of the workplace

Leaders have a crucial role as guardians of the psychological environment at work. They have the most influence to ensure that the workplace operates in psychologically aware, responsible, safe and healthy ways. Senior leaders must influence and shape the psychological landscape to make a workplace thrive. Leaders need to support others to flourish at the same time as supporting themselves. This is through prioritising what is good for everyone, not just themselves.

Regardless of who is functioning below the line, it is the role of leaders to enable and steward the psychological environment or ecosystem. By guiding the workplace culture, and everyone in it, to function above the line, leaders must maximise the environment to the benefit of everyone.

This can require examining the skills and strengths necessary for above-the-line functioning.

Who benefits from above-the-line leadership?

As your organisation and your people deserve and require the benefits of above-the-line leadership, leading above the line can be a game-changer in addressing many of the complicated and complex issues workplaces are struggling to solve.

I continue to speak with CEOs and senior leaders who are increasingly concerned with the time they and their teams spend fighting fires; therefore, taking too much focus and energy away from being innovative, visionary, strategic and future focused.

Whichever side of the line workplace interactions fall on, it will significantly influence performance, productivity, teamwork, engagement, the wellbeing of the workforce and the commitment of the workforce to their employer.

> The best leaders positively influence the psychological environment their workforce is marinating in each day.

So, what about Team Acacia?

Over a 9–12-month period, the senior leaders led the team to a massive upgrade in its psychological and interpersonal dynamics. The team became a sought-after employer in its service; it was fully staffed and its reputation was restored and even enhanced.

The senior leaders achieved this through work at three levels: leading themselves more effectively, leading their individual staff well and leading the team as a whole. They invested heavily in shifting their own behaviours above the line and committing to work more effectively as a team.

1. They were willing to explore the link between how they were leading themselves and the impact this had on their working relationships with each other. They had all become increasingly self-critical and could recognise how this profoundly impacted their ability to be appreciative and positive in their leadership approach. They became aware of their own narky behaviour and how they needed to build mindful awareness and to better self-manage

their frustrations. They stopped modelling poor behaviour such as playing favourites or using divide-and-conquer tactics, and began addressing some of the unproductive alliances they had developed as they grasped the toxic impact this was having on their team.

2. Through appreciating their strengths and skills and feeling support from each other, they became more strengths- and skills-focused in their interactions with their staff. This increased positive feedback and appreciation, and impacted performance and engagement. Their team members noted that they no longer felt under negative scrutiny, which freed them up to feel more relaxed and creative in their work.

3. Relationships within the team shifted significantly as the leaders began setting better boundaries, respectfully and kindly addressing below-the-line behaviours, explaining the impact and encouraging better interpersonal interactions. The leaders were far more aware of the fluctuations in the energy and climate of the team and could ramp up support at critical times.

Team Acacia is now functioning well above the line; it is being *productive* on its way to *peak*. When I met with the Team Acacia leaders for their final session, they described a significant impact on the level of service to their clients, which had prompted some innovations they were planning to present at a national conference.

They described the interpersonal impact as:

1. *Anyone can ask anyone for anything.* This showed they had built psychological safety; it was safe to ask for help from others.

2. *Everyone has everyone else's back.* This showed that everyone felt valued and connected; it was safe to be a team.

3. *Acacia team = mature wisdom + youthful energy.* All team members are valued for their unique contribution and are respected for what they bring.

4. We can be far more impactful when we bring a more systemic, strategic and holistic attitude. And it starts with you. It starts with how you lead yourself, your employees (and your relationship with your employees) and your team / workplace (the collective relationships).

IN SUMMARY

In this chapter, we discussed how the workplace functions as a psychological environment, where 'the line' is and how it can be influenced. We explored the differences in how workplaces can function from toxic to high performance and the ways in which these levels influence interpersonal relationships and dynamics.

In Chapter Three, we explore why leading ourselves above the line is the starting point for a psychologically responsible, high-performing team.

Questions for reflection:

As a leader, how do you tend to function in relation to the line?

When does your functioning drop below the line?

How do you shift yourself back above the line?

Who around you is excellent at staying above the line?

Who in your world regularly drops below the line?

What steps could you take to function more consistently above the line?

PART TWO

LEAD

Chapter Three

WHY LEAD YOURSELF ABOVE THE LINE?

*'Exceptional leaders distinguish themselves
because of superior self-leadership.'*
—Daniel Goleman

It is clear that we want our workplaces to operate above the line. When we lead our employees and teams to above-the-line functioning, there is one often neglected but critical step to address.

It starts, first and foremost, with leading you. Yes ... you.

We need to lead ourselves above the line before we can genuinely lead others above the line. Most leaders give scant attention to how they lead themselves, yet it is pivotal to how we lead others.

Leading yourself

Every time we speak to ourselves, we are building an internal relationship that can support or undermine us. Over time, this forms a template for other relationships. If we tend to be critical of ourselves, we'll likely be more critical of others.

Most people don't appreciate the impact we have on others when we don't lead ourselves well. Leaders who actively 'self-lead' above the line take ownership of their energy, personal responsibility and performance so they have a greater impact on others. Self-leaders who take high-level responsibility for themselves create an excellent high-performing work environment for their employees and teams.

Self-leaders create a climate that is psychologically safe and where relationships are built on respect and integrity. These relationships form the fertile ground upon which your organisation will flourish.

You can't lead others if you can't lead yourself

In his groundbreaking book, *Emotional Intelligence*, psychologist Daniel Goleman points out that the best leaders place significant attention on leading themselves.[60]

This notion is invaluable.

Yet, most of us are unaware that by actively leading ourselves, we will positively impact ourselves and our colleagues (and our loved ones too).

Conversely, poor self-leadership has a negative impact on ourselves, our relationships, our professional lives and our wellbeing. It leads us to operate below the line in ways that can be detrimental to us and / or those around us.

The COVID-19 pandemic has presented a profound opportunity for us all to lead ourselves and self-manage the complex situations we face.

In the next two chapters, I will explore and share:

- What is positive self-leadership?
- Why does above-the-line self-leadership matter?
- A framework to assist leaders to develop above-the-line self-leadership.
- Key insights into how to lead ourselves more strategically above the line.

Self-leadership is a vital skill set for the contemporary workplace

When we reflect on leadership, we primarily focus on how we want to be led by others or how we lead our employees. We think of leadership as an interpersonal relationship with others.

Self-leadership is an emerging concept that is still off the radar for many.

Self-leadership is leading yourself 'from the inside out'.

Self-leadership is the influence that individuals use to shape their own behaviours and thoughts.

Self-leadership is comprised of specific behavioural and cognitive strategies intended to increase personal effectiveness, mindset, performance and wellbeing.

> Self-leadership is self-awareness, self-direction and self-management.

According to self-leadership coach Andrew Bryant, 'Self-leadership is having a developed sense of who you are, what you can do, [and] where you are going, coupled with the ability to influence your communication, emotions, and behaviours on the way to getting there'.[61]

Self-leadership is an intra-personal relationship. We all have an internal relationship with ourselves, which, like all relationships, has different attributes, strengths, weaknesses, dynamics, patterns and habits. This intra-personal relationship reflects a psychological contract we have with ourselves and how we treat and relate to ourselves.

If our self-leadership relationship is positive, it helps us optimise our potential, and keep our energy high and our personal agency strong. Strong self-leaders are well anchored in their strengths, skills, capabilities, talents and values, and in their understanding of their meaning and purpose.

Positive self-leadership is a game-changing strategy that empowers people to regain control of their environment, achieve their potential and make a positive impact on those around them. It recognises that we cannot always remove the stressors, but we can build the agility, insight and energy to thrive.

Self-leadership can also be lacking—or, even worse, it can be at the negative end of the continuum.

Negative	Lacking	Positive

SELF-LEADERSHIP CONTINUUM

If one is lacking in self-leadership it is like a directionless boat: drifting rudderless, being pushed around by forces outside of its control. Psychologists call this having an external 'locus of control' because we are more determined by outside forces than by internal ones. If we lack self-leadership, we may neglect ourselves. This renders us more vulnerable to burnout and lack of fulfilment.

At the negative end of the continuum (if our self-leadership relationship is negative), it can be restrictive and de-energising, and it can undermine our goals and performance. Negative self-leadership means we are having an actively negative relationship with ourselves: speaking harshly to ourselves, judging and shaming ourselves or being actively self-sabotaging.

Questions for reflection:

How aware are you of your self-leadership?

How actively do you influence your self-leadership?

Self-leadership often remains outside our conscious awareness, where it is hard to conceptualise. As a result, a common pattern of self-leadership is that we inadvertently and unintentionally abrogate responsibility for leading ourselves to others. This results in negative or neglectful patterns of behaviour towards ourselves (below-the-line functioning).

Are you outsourcing your self-leadership?

As many of us value the concept of leadership, we expect (and hope) to be led by someone else and we certainly expect them to do it well.

Whether it's a manager, partner or family member, we often unintentionally outsource responsibility for self-leadership, believing it to be someone else's job to lead and maximise 'our' potential:

- Isn't that my manager's role?
- Isn't that my partner's responsibility?
- Isn't it my parents' job to help me be the best I can be?

If we have delegated that role, we may have likely delegated it without making the contract clear.

Ignoring the importance of leading ourselves can drive us to underestimate the negative impact poor self-leadership can have on ourselves and others. This is especially so when we lead ourselves far below the line in negative, dysfunctional or self-sabotaging ways.

What happens when we don't lead ourselves well?

Leading ourselves well is vital for sustainable peak performance. If we're not leading ourselves well, we'll neglect important elements like appreciating our strengths, skills, values, deeper needs or self-care. We won't take as much responsibility for the energy and presence we bring into our relationships. When we neglect self-leadership, we're likely to be disconnected from our skills, capabilities and potential. It also means we are more likely to project our unmet needs onto others, like our need for care, validation, worthiness, fulfilment and support.

> *'The cornerstone of effective leadership is self-mastery.'*
> —Patricia Aburdene

Negative self-leadership will complicate any relationship. This will be amplified when that dynamic is brought into a leadership role and workplace environment.

When we bring our unmet needs to the office, we unknowingly expect others to fulfil them. For example, we might continually seek out validation, attention, care or encouragement from others, rather than taking up our personal responsibility and ensuring we are providing that for ourselves.

Examples of below-the-line self-leadership

When people don't listen to themselves or are critical or self-neglectful, this is below-the-line self-leadership.

- When people don't listen to themselves, they continually seek to be heard by others.
- When people are self-critical, they may react badly to constructive feedback while dishing it out regularly. They might also be ultra-sensitive to others' opinions of them and put a large amount of energy into managing how others see them. Psychologists call this 'impression management'.
- When people neglect themselves, they are likely to feel annoyed or angry at others who they perceive as neglecting them. As self-neglect might also reflect low self-esteem, they may believe they deserve to be neglected.

How often do you hear people complain about their managers, with comments like, 'Oh, he spoke to me badly,' or 'She didn't listen to me,' or 'He dismissed me and my concerns,' or 'She criticised me'?

1. There is no excuse for bad leadership but if you dig a bit deeper, many of those complaining people would lead themselves far more negatively.
2. They speak to themselves more negatively than their manager speaks to them, and they do it 24/7.

3. They overly pick and fixate on the ways they don't live up to their own standards and expectations.

4. They notice their leader is behaving negatively towards them but they ignore the fact they may be doing exactly the same, or even worse, to themselves.

What word describes a common approach to self-leadership?

For many people, that word would be **self-criticism**.

If that is you, know that you are not alone. For most of us, it is so insidious, we don't even see how self-critical we are. Much of our self-criticism is when we critique our behaviours and words (what we did and said when in the presence of others). We may have said ten great things in a meeting but we'll tend to fixate on the one thing we could have said more effectively. Some of our self-criticism is focused on how we look and present ourselves to others. Common themes like not being good enough and not living up to a very high standard tend to dominate self-criticism.

If that is not you, then this is an opportunity to become aware of how the vast majority of the population functions. Most people are dealing with an unnecessary, unhelpful inner stream of self-criticism that affects how they navigate the world.

How can we protect ourselves from the harsh stream of negative criticism we subject ourselves to daily? We don't always have the self-awareness to hold ourselves accountable for the ongoing internal dialogue that is part of our relationship with ourselves.

Maybe we need stormtrooper gear to protect ourselves from ourselves.

How well are you leading yourself?

Let's take a moment to do two reflective exercises:

1. Reflect on the style of leadership that would bring out the best in you.

Which styles of leadership bring out the best in you?	
Disrespectful	Respectful
Defensive	Accountable
Unnecessarily critical	Committed to your learning and growth
Unreliable	Reliable
Blaming	Principled
Egocentric	Self-aware
Impatient	Consistent
Untrustworthy	Trustworthy
Manipulative	Appreciative
Harshly judgemental	Supportive
Micromanaging	Empowered
Bullying	Courageous
Mean-spirited	Generous
Controlling	Easygoing
Below-the-line leadership	Above-the-line leadership

I think I'm safe to assume all your ticks were in the right column.

2. Reflect on how you are leading yourself.

With which leadership style do you lead yourself currently?	
Disrespectful	Respectful
Harshly critical of self	Helpfully self-reflective
Overly focused on weaknesses, ignore strengths	Prioritise recognising strengths, see weakness as opportunities for growth
Doubt yourself	Back yourself

Below-the-line leadership	Above-the-line leadership
Easily blame and shame yourself	Work to reduce self-blame and shame patterns
Don't set boundaries	Good at boundaries, saying no as needed
Negative vibe towards yourself	Positive vibe towards yourself
Bullying yourself	Encouraging to self
Micromanaging of self	Empowering of self
Unreliable in your self-care	Reliable in your self-care
Mean-spirited to self	Generous to self
Self-denigrating	Self-compassionate

How did you go? Which column had the most ticks? What did you learn from this exercise?

When we lead ourselves well, we lead ourselves the way that we would:

a) expect to be led by our best leader

b) ideally lead our best employee.

If you are leading yourself below the line, you are impacting **yourself** in many ways:

- It may be harder to perform at your peak.
- It may reduce your ability to access your best thinking and decision-making.
- It may create mental and emotional exhaustion, and low energy.
- If you are not leading with your own values, you won't feel 'in alignment'.
- You're likely to feel more out of control.
- You're likely to get emotionally triggered more frequently.

- You may be more tuned in to what **others** think and want, and be inclined to roll over and let others' ideas dominate, rather than back yourself.
- It can lead to an increased risk of burnout.

If you are leading yourself below the line, you are also impacting **your colleagues:**

- They will miss out on you bringing your best self to work.
- They're more likely to experience your negative energy state.
- Your interactions with others will be energy draining.
- If you're highly critical of yourself, you're more likely to be highly critical of others (unless you are very high on empathy).
- You're likely to operate in automatic patterns and be less intentional.
- You may be less patient and more primed for conflict or combat.
- You'll get triggered more frequently, so you'll be less reliable, consistent and centred, and more reactive, stressed and overwhelmed.

When we lead ourselves above the line, we're empowered and take greater ownership of our own energy, mindset, behaviour and performance; therefore, we're likely to have a greater positive impact.

Meet Sarah (Ms Corporate Australia)

Sarah works in high-end retail. She has tens of thousands of employees who ultimately report to her.

When I first met Sarah she worked 6 days a week and gruelling 12-hour days and would describe her work persona as tense and a little snappy. Although she was kind, compassionate, cared deeply for her staff, and had exemplary values and intentions, she wasn't always able to act that way. She had many qualities of a great leader but was let down by her negative self-leadership.

Intentions were above the line, but behaviours were not

Sarah was loved by her staff members because they felt her care but they were disconcerted by her exacting standards and perfectionism. Although she was critical, she genuinely appreciated her employees' skills and talents.

There was a significant disconnect between how Sarah led herself and how she aimed to lead others. She was highly neglectful of her physical and mental health. She was exhausted, overwhelmed and distracted. Not only was her physical energy gutted, but her mental and emotional energy was non-existent.

Her perfectionistic standards were primarily directed towards herself. Her levels of self-criticism meant her head was not a place where you would want to hang out. She would unnecessarily ruminate over an endless list of what was wrong with her: her performance, relationships, future career prospects and her staff management.

This below-the-line style of self-leadership was HIGHLY impactful. It fed the more primitive parts of her brain; it kept her in a continual loop of negative thinking patterns, behaviours and interactions. Below-the-line self-leadership drastically reduced her bandwidth to lead others well.

Is it time to take charge of leading ourselves?

It never occurred to Sarah that she could lead herself in positive ways and work to bring out her best self. Like many people, she was inadvertently waiting for others to do this.

There are many contributing factors to why we haven't learned skills in self-leadership:

- We didn't have good role models in self-leadership.
- We were taught to meet others' expectations not our own, so fitting in with others was prioritised over being true to yourself.
- Many of us were not taught to trust ourselves, in fact, we may have been taught that trusting ourselves is dangerous and could lead us to bad things.
- Social conditioning in our family, school or culture may have focused us on being well-behaved, following the rules, respecting leaders and implicitly seeking external leadership.
- Tall poppy syndrome may have discouraged us from taking initiative.
- We learned to focus on what is wrong with us as the way to improve ourselves and never valued our skills, strengths or positive attributes.

Change starts with awareness

Sarah could tick a lot on the list. As she became aware of the impact of the negative patterns she was in, she decided not to give those contributing factors any more power over her life. She took the necessary steps to stop the vicious cycle.

Sarah's steps to leading herself above the line

Sarah's first step was to build **self-awareness** of her patterns of thinking and behaviour. Like many people, Sarah's continual self-critical pattern hijacked her ability to positively and constructively influence herself. For someone who has tremendous capacity to influence an organisation strategically, her ability to be intentionally influential with herself was, in contrast, very limited.

Self-criticism renders some of our usual capacities ineffective. Sarah learned to become familiar with her critical voice so she could influence and shape it. Some would say Sarah achieved a state of 'flawsome'—she could embrace her 'flaws' and appreciate she was awesome regardless.

Sarah's second step was to become more **self-directed**. She enhanced her personal agency through planning how to lead herself and live her life aligned to her values and aspirations while bringing out the best in herself. She could describe a life that was far more balanced and nourishing to her physical, mental and emotional wellbeing. She realised that this would ensure she could perform more effectively and be able to provide better leadership to her direct reports.

And her third step was about building **self-management** through consolidating and managing her tendency to fall back into old habits during times of stress. Although she made considerable progress, Sarah found that at several points she regressed into old habits. Learning to manage herself better involved having a deeper awareness of what preceded those times and the signposts that were important to heed.

In this way, these setbacks were invaluable learning moments for Sarah, as she learnt not just how to move forward and ahead but also how to catch herself and support herself during the toughest times.

This learning created a lot more sustainability.

One of the most powerful shifts for Sarah was how she began to deeply relax.

Constant self-criticism and perfectionism hold us hostage to stress and reptile brain functioning. We don't feel psychologically safe with ourselves.

Organisations need capable self-leaders

The benefits of above-the-line self-leadership are not just for you and your team. Organisations desperately need above-the-line self-leading employees who are empowered to take control of their own success and performance, and who aren't waiting to be led by others.

Research shows that self-leaders are a huge asset to any workplace; they propel organisations forward, and build capacity and agility.[62] Self-leaders cope better with change and challenge because they see them as opportunities for growth—a clear advantage in navigating the year 2020.

Building self-leadership awareness and skills leads to greater organisational success because it empowers people to regain control of their direction, to fulfil their potential and to make a positive impact on others around them.

Fortunately, like in Sarah's case, self-leadership can be developed. It requires a willingness to engage, but increasing productivity and positivity is an inspiring motivator for anyone.

In fact, self-leadership underpins a mentally healthy workplace. It creates a psychologically healthy foundation for individuals and an entire workforce.

Sweden's public service: A self-leadership innovator

In 2014, Sweden's public sector moved to a model of self-leadership to deal with hierarchical and management issues and to help maximise its performance.

This program has had significant research outcomes. The results show that employees work more collaboratively, with more unity and clearer direction, and have greater confidence and security.[63]

Another important lesson the research identified was that change needs to be driven by the senior management team but has to involve the whole organisation from the outset. Commitment, ownership and patience are required. It is understood that self-leadership is a skill set that needs to be continually developed in daily work routines.

IN SUMMARY

We can see that leading yourself above the line provides a strong foundation for your capacity to lead yourself and others well. Self-leadership is an emerging concept that encourages us to apply the same principles, values and leadership practices to leading ourselves that we would use to lead others. We understand that the key elements of the relationship we each have with ourselves is equal to the psychological contract we are operating within and that, for the most part, this remains outside of our awareness.

In Chapter Four, we will explore several approaches and strategies we can utilise to build the foundation upon which we will lead ourselves above the line. We will carry out the practical steps to becoming an exemplary self-leader.

Questions for reflection:

How would you lead and support your best employee?

What steps would you take? What approach would you use?

How would you want to help them be the best contributors and bring out their talent?

How do you want to show up?

As a leader, what do you want to model for your employees?

How do your answers guide how you might like to lead yourself?

Chapter Four

HOW TO LEAD YOURSELF
ABOVE THE LINE

*There's only one corner of the universe
you can be certain of improving,
and that's your own self.'*
—Aldous Huxley

Positive self-leadership

Developing above-the-line self-leadership requires building and cultivating a realistic relationship with ourselves. Having a positive relationship with ourselves is not about living in narcissistic la-la land; it means accepting ourselves, our strengths and our challenges, living in alignment with our values and goals, and learning to manage ourselves in ways that optimise our potential.

Leading ourselves well means finding a level of self-acceptance that does not require us to be perfect at one end of the continuum and worthless at the other. Instead, we find ways to be more self-accepting and create space inside for our strengths, vulnerabilities, quirkiness, goals, dreams, potential, and our opportunities for growth and development.

Leading ourselves above the line may mean reducing the double standards where we treat others better than we treat ourselves. Many people, but not everyone, treat others far better than they treat themselves.

For those who are more inclined to be arrogant and egocentric, good self-leadership may mean coming to terms with their limitations and humanity, which could result in treating others more equally and fairly.

Questions for reflection:

How would you want your loved ones to treat themselves? Harshly or kindly?

What guiding principles would you want them to apply to bring out the best in themselves?

Self-leaders navigate life and work from the inside out. They strategically work towards a future that is defined by values, intentions and hopes in ways that maximise their talent and the potential of others.

Leading yourself above the line unleashes potential. When you are run by your below-the-line reptile brain, you inadvertently and unconsciously limit your strengths and capacities. You keep yourself small. Positive self-leaders bring a more empowering above-the-line approach to their workplace.

During the COVID-19 pandemic, positive self-leadership has been an incredible asset. Strong self-leaders have found it easier to accept the situation, adapt their standards and expectations, and adjust to finding ways to be centred and maintain productivity. They have brought a kinder, less narky version of themselves to their relationships.

Self-leaders are authentic; they generate positivity and productivity for their colleagues. They function mostly from the executive brain; therefore, thinking skills are maximised as they have the capacity to be strategic, creative and innovative. Their cognitive and psychological agility enables them to see situations from other people's perspectives. This gives them an edge in minimising conflict and maximising team productivity. Self-leaders shine under stress; they use a high level of self-mastery to maintain their centre in a storm, navigating themselves back to a positive mindset during challenges.

How do we develop self-leadership skills?

A. **The short answer** is lead yourself the way you would want to be led by someone else.

No-one can tell you what you need to do to be the best leader of yourself.

You know which leadership approach brings out the best in you when being led by someone else.

Questions for reflection (about your ideal leader):

How would they build a good relationship with you?

What steps would they take to bring out the best in you?

How would they support you?

How would they give you feedback?

How would they approach you when you make mistakes or when you need to learn skills you have not yet mastered?

How would they approach you when you're overwhelmed?

Make some notes about your answers. Can you turn these into tips for leading yourself?

*'Self-leadership is the greatest
leadership challenge.'*
—John Maxwell

B. **For the longer answer**, we'll delve into ways to apply your most important leadership principles for leading yourself.

Leading yourself above the line involves taking greater psychological responsibility for yourself, for how you show up in the world and by doing what you can to be your best. This involves stepping through three key elements: self-awareness is the foundation for self-direction, which is the foundation for self-management.

1. Self-awareness

2. Self-direction

3. Self-management

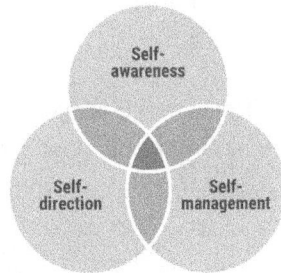

There are many pathways to achieve this and there is definitely no one-size-fits-all approach. This chapter explores the various steps to strengthen self-leadership that arise from research-based evidence. Please see them as a smorgasbord of strategies and implement one or two that resonate with you most.

Step 1: Self-awareness

Greater self-awareness is the first step to building self-leadership. As the foundation for optimising our functioning, it is an exceptional above-the-line and psychologically responsible step we can take to bring our best selves to work.

Self-awareness is a foundational skill of emotional intelligence (EI). It helps us:

- recognise and examine the influences on our behaviours, patterns, biases and values
- become aware of and build on our strengths and skills
- identify potential areas for development and make changes as needed
- provide the groundwork to enable us to align behaviours with values and intentions, which is the key for leading ourselves above the line
- navigate interpersonal relationships, build trust and find opportunities to work together with others to maximise outcomes.

The barriers to self-awareness can be complex. Both unnecessary self-criticism and being overly concerned with others' expectations can disconnect us from knowing and understanding ourselves in a helpful way. What often drives these unconstructive habits of thinking is a deeper need for acceptance and validation.

Impact of external opinions

Being overly tuned in to how others see us limits self-awareness. This occurs when we perceive ourselves through other people's perspectives and expectations. For most people, this is off the radar. As a method, we are often more focused on meeting others' expectations. We unconsciously use this to gain acceptance and validation. This external focus takes us away from developing our potential and reinforces the drive to fit in with others and their expectations. We can see that this seriously cramps our style and hinders the possibility of stepping more fully into aspects of our potential.

*'The definition of hell: On your last day
on earth, the person you became will
meet the person you could have become.'*

—Anonymous

Living up to everyone's expectations can create internal conflict as others' expectations are not always going to align with your own. To harness your own potential, you need to build a solid foundation of internal harmony. This happens when there is internal alignment between your values, your thoughts, your actions and your goals.

For Sarah, who we met in Chapter Three, this was a huge key to self-awareness and growth. She became aware of how she was caught up trying to meet others' expectations. Interestingly, though, when we explored this in more depth, she had actually created stories about what others expected of her that were often 'perceived expectations' and not based in reality. These perceived expectations created many 'shoulds' that hounded her and fuelled an unnecessarily harsh level of self-criticism when she was unable to live up to these overwhelming 'perceived expectations'.

Self-critical behaviour

Reduce self-criticism and build self-reflection

One of the biggest challenges to harnessing your own potential is the incessant level of self-criticism many of us are habitually engaged in for significant amounts of time each day. My 'anecdata' (anecdotal data) suggests that most people habitually criticise themselves; they overly focus on their perceived limitations and fail to recognise their strengths, skills and capacities.

Reducing unnecessary self-criticism is about building a deeper level of self-awareness that can enable us to more powerfully build on our limitations and grow. Reducing self-criticism is a powerful step in leading oneself above the line.

Research shows that we have a negativity bias (this, in the past, was necessary for survival).[64] However, we know that the entrenched patterns of self-criticism are damaging to our mental and psychological wellbeing, cognitive and psychological agility, productivity, relationships and energy.

From what we have explored regarding brain wiring, continually thinking negatively about yourself reinforces fear-based and negatively biased thought patterns. It strengthens the pathways to the reptile brain, so our attention will default to noticing negatives and weaknesses. This focused attention on the negative means we'll have far more words for weaknesses and limitations.

Some of us have mistakenly come to believe that we won't get ahead without being self-critical. We're afraid of being kind or compassionate to ourselves; we worry this will somehow lead to self-indulgence or we'll lose compassion for others.

Your capacity for constructive self-reflection is vital. Please know from the get-go that reducing self-criticism is not about pandering to ourselves or becoming blind to our limitations and learning edges. In fact, it is the opposite. When we continually self-criticise, we prevent ourselves from being self-reflective and addressing some of our perceived limitations.

Questions for self-reflection:

Write a list of your top ten strengths and a list of your top ten weaknesses.

Which was quicker to do?

Most people tell me the weaknesses could be done quickly but it might take them a few weeks to write ten strengths. Can you relate to this?

Self-critical behaviour leads us to develop a skewed awareness of ourselves and may be a huge factor in imposter syndrome. Imposter syndrome is where we are so unaware of our strengths and so aware of our limitations that we feel undeserving of our success—we feel like a fraud. Being overly self-critical significantly constrains us from recognising and developing our potential.

If we're self-critical, we're likely to be critical of others too. If our relationship template is that we're negative towards ourselves, this is how we'll relate to others. Now, you might be thinking you're very critical of yourself, but not so critical of others. If this is the case, this tells me you are high on empathy. Empathy can be a mediating factor. If you are high on empathy but highly self-critical, you're less likely to unleash your inner critical voice on the outer world. However, if you are low on empathy, your colleagues and loved ones probably bear the brunt of your critical perspective, which, if not censored, can be like a weapon of mass destruction.

When we are less self-critical, we are far more present and less preoccupied in our head, so our capacity to listen deeply grows exponentially. Once we reduce self-criticism and deepen self-understanding, we're more strategic in building self-leadership and self-management.

Top tips to reduce self-criticism:

1. First, become aware of your critical voice. What does it say to you repeatedly? You may have been told that you are too _____ (fill in the blank). This becomes your critical voice and you tell yourself 'that' thing over and over. For me, it was that I was too sensitive, too meaty (my Hungarian grandmother's word for chubby), too loud, too happy. Such a destructive voice IS poor self-leadership. Would you speak like that to anyone else?

2. Give your critical voice a name like Negative Nancy or Tyrannical Tyrone and observe when they are more present.

3. Try to notice the patterns. Keep sticky note reminders in places where you spend quiet moments, like on the bathroom mirror for when you are brushing your teeth. Review how you have been going with your 'reduce self-criticism project' each day.

4. Remind yourself to speak to you the way you would speak to someone you care about. Practise speaking to yourself how you would speak to a good friend or family member. What qualities would you bring? Humour? Respect? Encouragement? Support? Apply those to yourself.

Remember that harsh self-criticism is quite counterproductive to awareness and development. Shaming yourself does not support change; it reinforces your negative thinking patterns.

*'Simple kindness to one's self and
all that lives is the most powerful
transformational force of all. It produces
no backlash, has no downside, and never
leads to loss or despair. It increases one's
own true power without exacting any toll.'*
—Dr. David Hawkins MD. PhD

Build appreciation of your strengths and skills

Building on your potential involves knowing and understanding your own strengths, values, preferences, talents and wisdom. If you start to reduce the pattern of being overly self-critical, like Sarah did, your awareness of your skills, values and talents will develop.

We have limited language about strengths and skills. The habit of harsh self-criticism, for most people, has created an imbalance where they are skilled in detecting and languaging weaknesses. Our internal judging voice has been so busy, it's developed a PhD. We can criticise ourselves and others. Research highlights that most employees receive specific feedback about their weaknesses, but when it comes to the positives (strengths and skills), most of us receive very little specific feedback.[65] We mostly receive feedback based on effort or outcome. This is great, but it's just not helpful enough.

So, one of the challenges we have is to develop a strength- and skill-based language to make this flow more naturally. This, like all of the other skills we are exploring, will be vital when it comes to giving feedback to others.

There are many ways to fast-track this. Here are some examples:

1. Discover your strengths. There is a range of surveys that provide insights into strengths including the VIA Character Strengths survey, Strengthscope and the Clifton StrengthsFinder. Write your strengths down and regularly review how you use them at work and at home.

2. Seek positive feedback from (trusted) others. Choose three people whom you trust and respect. Ask if they would be willing to put aside time to give you feedback about your top five strengths. Give them time to reflect on these, and when you meet to hear the feedback, note it down and review it regularly. Add to this, over time, with the positive feedback and compliments you receive.

3. Make it a daily practice to write down three skills or strengths you used during the past 24 hours. Particularly look for strengths and skills drawn from:

   - personal capacities
   - interpersonal skills
   - emotional intelligence
   - collaboration and teamwork skills
   - cognitive skills like being strategic, thinking laterally or being innovative
   - leadership
   - professional and technical competencies
   - conflict and negotiation skills
   - self-leadership and self-management
   - skills of efficiency, routine, structure
   - skills of strategy, creativity, innovation
   - ethics and fairness.

4. Brainstorm a potential list of skills that you value and recognise in others.

Step 2: Self-direction

'You are your own leader. Where are you driving yourself to now? You can't afford to go wayward! Rise up and break new territories and live life so well.'

—Israelmore Ayivor

In life, we are guided by a combination of our values, goals, dreams and hopes, and we are influenced by a set of external expectations and demands. These internal and external drivers are under continual renegotiation. If we believe we're driven by external forces and not anchored into our inner drivers, our locus of control is external.

What I notice in many leaders is how 'external' their locus of control has become. The overwhelm that many leaders express reflects that they feel and believe they are not fully in the driver's seat of their own lives. Leaders often describe how their professional and personal demands have swamped their resources and that they are not at a preferable level of self-determination.

The stages to building self-directedness involve stepping more fully into your personal agency and authority—authority over your own life (and not being controlled by others).

Building self-direction starts with clarity about your values. This will guide your direction and efforts.

Develop clarity about your values

Your values are non-negotiable; they are an important part of who you are and how you navigate the world. If you are not sure of your values, there are many ways to gain a deeper understanding of them. Simon Sinek's TED talk and book, *Start with Why*, shines a powerful light on the importance of understanding our 'why': what gives us meaning and purpose.[66,67]

Throughout this book, my own 'why' may be evident. I'm highly motivated by helping leaders build relationships and cultures that are psychologically responsible. When culture is not psychologically responsible, employee potential is squandered.

Questions for reflection:

What are your values?

What is your 'why'?

What motivates you?

There are many 'value' checklists available online that can assist.

Gandhi said, 'Happiness is when what you think, what you say and what you do are in harmony'.[68] Perhaps strong self-leadership is when what you value, your intentions and your actions are in harmony.

Shape your thinking patterns and your relationship with yourself

Above-the-line self-leadership involves taking charge of your thinking patterns to ensure that your thoughts are not negatively skewed. If your patterns of thinking have a continual negative orientation, this undercurrent will always push you in one direction, no matter how hard you swim against the tide.

'Negative thoughts are like Velcro,
positive thoughts are like Teflon.'
—Rick Hanson

We tend to believe that our thinking patterns are fixed—a little like highways that can't be moved without years of intense work. Luckily for us, advances in technology have shown that our brains and their neural pathways are far more flexible and plastic than we realised.

Although it can take a little time and effort, the field of neuroplasticity provides clear evidence that through intentionally choosing to think different thoughts, we can actively influence the underlying wiring of our brain.[69,70] This is called 'positive neuroplasticity'.[71] Our need for survival has given us a negativity bias. However, we don't need to allow negative default thinking patterns to be automatic and shape our brain in ways that hijack us.

One great way to change this is to become aware of our thoughts as they are happening. This is where we use self-awareness and then self-direction to make different choices about our thought patterns. Many of my clients have benefited from seeing mistakes or errors as learning opportunities. When something does not go well, they have learned to ask themselves the question: What can I learn from this? This is far more helpful than starting a narrative of not being good enough. Making this shift gets easier over time; the more you practise, the easier it happens.

Another favourite quote from Rick Hanson that reflects positive neuroplasticity and cognitive bias is, 'When things go well, we attribute it externally. When things are not going well, we attribute it to our own shortcomings'.[72] This highlights the impact of default thinking patterns.

If we choose to be aware of our thinking patterns and preference positive patterns, we are more likely to notice the positive. Doing this regularly literally rewires our brain. It is called self-directed positive neuroplasticity, and it is a powerful way to lead ourselves to a better future.

Here are some ways to apply the research from positive neuroplasticity[73,74]:

- Absorb the good: Look for good things in your day and your world and let them become good experiences. Savour positive emotions and experiences for at least ten seconds, or more, to help your brain get the benefits.
- Be aware of your thinking habits and patterns: Create reminders to regularly redirect your thoughts to the positive. Set reminders on your phone, or place sticky notes on your bathroom mirror or on your desk at work.
- Practise deep breathing, mindfulness or meditation, if it works for you.

There are excellent apps that can help. You can try Calm, Smiling Mind, Headspace or Insight Timer. You can use these to disconnect from the pressures of the day. Even 15 seconds several times a day can be beneficial. Mindfulness and meditation are not for everyone. If you struggle with these practices but are keen to use them, seek out an expert who can help you find the right approach for you. This may be especially important if you've had a lot of life difficulties, anxieties or trauma.

Be open to feedback and lifelong learning

How do you like to learn? How comfortable are you with growth and development?

Personally, I believe that openness to lifelong learning and development is the elixir of youth. When we shut down to learning, we stop growing and may put a lot of energy into shutting off to new ideas and innovation. The people I know who are closed to learning are often arrogant and defensive and look for fault in others.

We all need an ego to have self-belief and conviction, yet too much of a good thing can be detrimental to our openness to growth and learning. This is especially so when our ego dominates our work persona. Harnessing our ego means allowing it to support us to appreciate our value and, at the same time, enabling us to be open to learning. This is an important intersection where we can honour our strengths, skills and value, and be aware of our need for growth and development.

Our capacity to be open to feedback and appreciate that we are all works in progress, both professionally and personally, is essential.

> *'Waking up to who you are requires letting go of who you imagine yourself to be.'*
> —Alan Watts

Here are some useful strategies to try:

- Look for learning opportunities every day. What can each interaction with others teach you? Even those you don't respect or like can teach you something—even if it is how you don't want to show up in the world.

- Seek out feedback from those you trust.
- Be open to the gems that may be present in everyone's feedback.
- Cultivate your own self-assessment skills.
- Seek out opportunities to do something new. Being a beginner is humbling and helpful to our ego management.

Step 3: Self-management

> *'Self-management ... is all about becoming your own leader by training your mental, physical, social and intellectual faculties in different ways.'*
> —Dr Prem Jagyasi

Manage yourself through managing your mojo and your triggers. Your mojo is influenced by how you manage your energy state and how you deal with your triggers.

Your energy state is the vibe or energy you bring into every situation. When you function above the line, you have awareness of your energy state. This moment-by-moment attention to how you navigate your day is a self-leadership superpower that enables you to influence your way to above-the-line self-leadership.

Manage your energy state

> *'Don't ask what the world needs. Ask*
> *what makes you come alive, and go*
> *do it. Because what the world needs*
> *is people who have come alive.'*
> —Howard Thurman

A good example of leading with my energy state came up this morning. I was finding it quite challenging to settle down and write this chapter. There is a townhouse development happening next door, and at 7 am each morning, four metres from where I sit and work, there is noise from a ghetto-blaster and building equipment. It was not having a good impact on my energy and could have easily led me along a below-the-line pathway to feeling frustrated and giving up on my writing for the day. Instead, I took the above-the-line pathway. I decided to play some energising music, and a few minutes later, I was dancing around the house and ready to sit down at the keyboard. I made great progress. As you can see, awareness of your state and the ability to influence it has a significant impact on you, your productivity and how to show up in all of your relationships.

To function at our peak, we need good health and energy. We benefit from wholesome self-care practices that allow us to perform well under pressure and have the energy to engage fully in both our professional and personal lives. We need enough physical, mental, emotional and spiritual energy (please leave out spiritual or soulful if it is not important to you) to bring out the best in ourselves and to have enough energy to deal with what is on our plate.

When we have adequate energy levels, we can attend to the things we *have* to do, as well as to the things we *want* to do. We can invest in ourselves, our wellbeing, our relationships, our meaningful activities, our interests, our career and our future. If our energy is depleted, then even ordering Uber Eats for dinner can be too taxing a job.

> Make yourself a priority often enough so you bring your best self to the world always.

We also benefit from learning to manage our energy state and vibe, and understanding that how we show up in the world influences our daily experience as well as our relationships with others.

Every morning, as we get ready for our workday, we prepare our physical bodies in terms of our appearance, but we don't usually give enough thought to how we prepare our physical, mental and emotional energy. Yet, how we experience our day and how others experience us will be far more dependent on our energy than the clothes we choose to wear (unless we choose stormtrooper gear ☺).

Here is an exercise to help manage your energy state:

Brainstorm small things that you can do each day to save and build your energy. Here are some examples:

Save energy	Build energy
Less harsh self-criticism.	Eat well, drink enough water.
Less shame and guilt storms.	Fresh air for a few minutes at lunchtime.
Avoid energy vampires at the office or at home: people who are gossipy, bitchy and negative.	Add fun and humour during breaks.
Less junk / diet food.	Listen to energising music to and from work.
Less TV, social media or computer games.	Deep breathing: five deep breaths, five times per day.
Less clutter.	Daily gratitude practice.
Less unreasonable and excessive demands.	Absorb and savour the good.
	Give one colleague a compliment each day.

Try some strategies that boost and save your energy, and assess what helps keep your energy more sustainable.

'People look for retreats for themselves, in the country, by the coast, or in the hills. There is nowhere that a person can find a more peaceful and trouble-free retreat than in his own mind. So constantly give yourself this retreat, and renew yourself.'
—Marcus Aurelius

Manage your triggers

One of the most challenging aspects of leading ourselves above the line on an ongoing basis is managing our reptile brain, particularly when we get emotionally triggered. We can be triggered by many situations. When our executive brain is offline, we are hijacked by the more primitive and reactive parts of our brain.

This happens to all of us. The timing of our triggers is unpredictable and can take us by surprise. In those moments (when our reptile brain reacts to some perceived threat or stress), our executive brain is hard to access, and so we're forced into a reactive fight or flight mode.

When we get triggered, we're inclined to be reactive and defensive, to place blame and to take our frustrations out on others. How we manage ourselves when we are triggered becomes extremely important as we can cause a lot of interpersonal damage in workplace relationships. If we are reactive and behave out of character, it can erode trust and credibility. We may be perceived as less dependable or reliable.

When we've learned to manage our triggers, it's easier to keep our behaviour aligned with our values, or the values of the workplace, rather than discharging the emotion or frustration. Managing our triggers optimises our functioning, productivity and performance.

At work, self-managing helps us perform more effectively under pressure. It helps us adapt to the changes that are thrown our way on a daily basis. We need more employees and leaders who can self-manage and navigate distractions, competing needs and demands.

It is especially important to learn how to positively influence our brain, deal with our own triggers and elevate our functioning from our reptile reflexes. This involves taking responsibility for influencing our patterns of thinking and behaviour, and ensuring we use this to perform more effectively. It is comprised of specific behavioural (doing) and cognitive (thinking) strategies that are intended to maintain personal effectiveness and performance.

Good self-management gives us the agility and adaptability necessary to lead ourselves well. We begin with awareness, we build direction and leadership and then we build management. In order to manage ourselves well, we need awareness, and we need to know where we want to be.

We can learn to be strategic with ourselves so that when we're triggered, we have well-established routines to guide ourselves. When we recognise that we are *getting into a thinking pattern* or *getting reactive because of that person* or *getting envious or angry,* we have a plan of action that will help us navigate those times more effectively.

If we get physically sick with a headache or a stomach upset, we know what to do. We have established patterns of how we support ourselves through those physical challenges. But mental support is less developed in most of us.

Here are some examples of strategies for dealing with your triggers:

- Do some physical activity; take a walk or do some form of exercise.
- Take ten deep breaths.
- Write down how you are feeling.
- Find somewhere you can speak loudly (like your car) and express all your frustrations aloud.
- Sing loudly out of earshot of others.
- Craft a playlist of music for stressful times that helps you release the energy that is sustaining your triggers. I

personally find rock music (think Rolling Stones, Santana, Dire Straits) to be perfect, but now I am showing my age.

- Build an emotional or mental first aid kit. This could be a list on your phone or at home that reminds you of the steps you can take to feel better when you are feeling triggered. I have links on my phone for blogs that make me laugh at myself and help me shift my energy.

What works for you? Write down a plan, and next time you are triggered, try those things and see how they help.

IN SUMMARY

In this chapter, we discussed how creating a thriving workplace and ecosystem depends on our ability to lead ourselves, and align our values and expectations to what we know to be positive. We reflected on the premise that leading ourselves well ensures we'll have the template for how to lead others well.

Self-leaders create a climate that is psychologically safe and relationships that are built on respect and integrity. This forms the fertile ground for an organisation to flourish.

In Chapter Five, we will explore how we can use our foundation of self-leadership to build strong interpersonal relationships with our employees.

Questions for reflection:

What steps can you take to build time for self-reflection?

How self-critical are you? Does your self-criticism get in the way of appreciating your strengths?

How regularly do you make time to be clear on and review your values?

How engaged are you in being a lifelong learner?

How can you better manage your energy state?

What steps can you take to manage your reptile brain and triggers?

Chapter Five

WHY LEAD YOUR EMPLOYEES ABOVE THE LINE?

'No one cares how much you know,
until they know how much you care.'
—Theodore Roosevelt

Employees are impacted by the relationship they have with their leader or manager. In our life experience, we know there are pivotal relationships that can significantly impact our wellbeing— our relationship with our direct line manager is one of those. It can be positive or poisonous or anywhere in between.

Our relationships at work (and in particular our relationship with our line manager) will considerably impact performance. Interpersonal neurobiology shines a light on how this occurs. If you are often in fear at work, the neural pathways to the primitive parts of the brain will become reinforced, making it harder to access your higher cognitive and psychological functioning.

The individual relationships you build with your employees will literally impact the wiring of their brains (as discussed in Chapter Two). There is a long-term impact here. The fear or strain generated from poor leadership will influence and activate your reptile brain, making it harder to optimise your executive brain functioning. End result: it will be harder to think clearly and relax, and to be creative, optimistic and strategic.

Meet Anna and Jasmine

Anna recently sought coaching after several challenges with her new manager, Jasmine. Anna has worked for 20 years in the same organisation where her specialised technical skills and contribution to teamwork are highly valued.

She loves her role so much that she never pursued promotions or other positions. Her previous manager, Joe, was an excellent mentor. He gave her lots of positive feedback and encouraged her to take the level of autonomy necessary for her specialist role. His constructive guidance helped her develop exceptional skills and he supported her organisational commitment.

As a technical expert, Anna carries high-level responsibility for her employer's customers. She works long hours and stays back late, when required, to troubleshoot time-critical issues. After staying back several hours on an emergency situation, Jasmine ticked Anna off disrespectfully and publicly when she arrived at work the next day because she was three minutes past her official starting time. These three minutes were completely inconsequential as far as the functioning of the workplace went; she was not late for a meeting or deadline.

Below-the-line behaviours

After other similar issues occurred, Anna respectfully tried to raise her concerns privately with Jasmine. However, Jasmine was unwilling to listen to Anna's concerns; she rolled her eyes and quickly shut the conversation down.

This is a common example of leading below the line.

What below-the-line behaviours did you notice in Jasmine?

- Public shaming and disrespect?
- Being unnecessarily critical of Anna?
- Being unwilling to listen to Anna's concerns?
- Demeaning behaviour like eye-rolling?

- Asking an employee to carry high-level responsibility and then undermine their basic autonomy?

Jasmine's behaviour was not only awful towards Anna but as her behaviour was in a shared workspace, it modelled toxic interpersonal behaviour to everyone in the vicinity. These interactions change everyone's conduct. It says to everyone present (and even those who were not) that *public shaming and disrespect is acceptable here*. It shifts the boundaries of what is deemed as acceptable and reasonable, and it shifts the psychological contract downwards to include disrespect and shaming.

What is the impact of below-the-line behaviours on employees?

When below-the-line behaviours occur, everyone in the vicinity feels unsafe—whether they are aware of it or not. People are instinctively more on guard and self-protective. Their radar gets triggered and they understandably wonder, *will it be me next?* Even worse, when the going gets tough and employees are under stress, they're more likely to follow suit and behave badly too.

Questions for reflection:

How does the interpersonal behaviour in your workplace influence you and your colleagues?

What are some of the worst below-the-line workplace behaviours you have witnessed?

What are some of the most powerful above-the-line behaviours you have observed?

Who do you notice to be always / mostly functioning above the line?

Who do you notice to sometimes function below the line?

From a brain (neuroscientific) perspective, we can see that Jasmine's conduct fed the reptile brain of anyone who was present.

An active reptile brain diminishes performance and engagement

When employees like Anna are subject to below-the-line behaviours, they tend to feel unsafe, devalued and disconnected. This is problematic. There is ample evidence to show that being on the receiving end of such below-the-line behaviours will prompt flight, fight or freeze patterns and release the stress hormones cortisol and adrenaline.[75,76,77]

As a result of Jasmine's behaviour, Anna's colleagues might observe a noticeable change in Anna's demeanour and performance. Jasmine's below-the-line behaviour would feed Anna's reptile brain, rendering her to underperform and become increasingly ineffective in her role. The stress of this situation may lead Anna to withdraw and feel humiliated and isolated. If Jasmine's below-the-line behaviour is ongoing, it has the potential to negatively impact Anna's workplace engagement, her performance and productivity and, ultimately, her mental health and wellbeing.

In these circumstances, most people will become more dominated by the reptile brain that limits their ability to think clearly and function well interpersonally. The workplace will not get the benefits of one's best skills, competencies and insights.

The power of leaders

The relationships we have with our leaders and managers are pivotal to how we experience our roles at work. Research shows that people leave and quit their managers more so than their roles or workplace.[78]

> Every interaction at work has the potential to support or undermine employees' performance, productivity, engagement and wellbeing.

Interpersonal interactions are central to how employees experience their workplace. These interactions influence their commitment and engagement.

Leaders and managers who take responsibility for the psychological impact of their interactions with employees are highly emotionally intelligent and positively powerful. As was evidenced in Jasmine's behaviour and the extensive research quoted in Chapter One, not enough leaders take this high level of psychological responsibility.

'When I talk to managers, I get the feeling they're important. When I talk to leaders, I get the feeling I'm important.'
—Alexander den Heijer

Relationships directly shape the wiring of our brains

This sobering fact emphasises the way our relationships at work dramatically impact our neural wiring and work performance in both short- and long-term ways. The emerging area of interpersonal neurobiology highlights that interpersonal relationships and our psychological environment shape our brain and its functioning.

This is one hell of a responsibility for every leader and manager. I'm sure you can also relate to how impactful this can be.

An above-the-line leader brings out the best in each of us, and not just during the day—the impact is enduring. If you are lucky to have an above-the-line leader, you're more likely to go home feeling positive and optimistic, and you'll sleep better and have more energy for your personal life. The positive impact means you'll be more engaged, energised and optimistic in ways that reinforce neural pathways to your executive brain. These help you perform better at work and manage your stressors far more effectively.

A below-the-line leader has the opposite impact. After each day in the office, you're far more likely to be exhausted and worn out, and to carry the strain and negativity home. The fear and negativity generated actually impacts your brain; it reinforces the wiring to your reptile brain and makes it harder to manage your stressors and challenges. You're more likely to feel overwhelmed. Research also shows that a poor leader can have a negative impact on your sleep and your partner's sleep too.[79,80,81]

Below-the-line management was the norm

In the past, managers deployed fear and control tactics to coerce employees to get into line. Many of these toxic behaviours were modelled in our homes and schools. Fear was frequently used as an external motivator to get people to work hard. Mostly, this was when employees worked on practical tasks that required physical effort, not higher order thinking, complex problem-solving or positive relationships with customers or within teams.

When we did not need to use our brains much, other than for performing the most rudimentary duties, fear may have been a successful, yet highly toxic, driver.

However, in our contemporary world, where employees must access their highest cognitive functions, fear has a seriously detrimental effect. It locks away one's best abilities behind an inaccessible firewall. While our reptile brain is activated, it interferes with our ability to think and function well and to successfully navigate customer or collegial relationships. This makes our working day exhausting as we have to concentrate extremely hard to fulfil our work requirements while we have less access to our best thinking.

Have we left these below-the-line approaches behind?

Although we have come a long way in recognising that fear-based motivators / drivers are counterproductive (even damaging and toxic), they are still common. Perhaps the hardest part of eliminating them from our workplaces is how deeply unaware we are of them, and how blind we are to how we use fear and shame as motivators.

Human motivation at work

As humans, we have our own internal and intrinsic motivators. When we want to draw the best out of employees, it is far more strategic to mobilise intrinsic positive motivators than to drive people to work hard through fear. If we value and need employees who think well, who are strategic, lateral and creative, and who are able to navigate interpersonal relationships well, we need to banish fear from our motivational toolbox. Fear is a below-the-line strategy.

As humans, we go to work for many reasons. Most employees have intrinsic motivations to gain mastery and meaning through their professional roles. Given that we go to work to make a life and a living, we optimise this time through allowing work to contribute to fulfilling our essential human needs. These include:

- to be our best selves, to feel we make a positive difference
- to give ourselves and our families the best lives
- to fulfil our potential and thrive
- to learn, grow and develop professionally and personally
- to connect with others and have a sense of belonging with our team and colleagues.

Above-the-line leaders understand and take into account the interpersonal impact of their behaviours on the people they lead. They also recognise that these essential needs are vital for every employee.

In the workplace, we need employees who are engaged, innovative, creative and enthusiastic in order for them to perform well. We need employees who are motivated to contribute beyond what is required in their roles. We observed Anna who was a valued asset in her workplace, a committed, loyal and hardworking employee who went above and beyond to address the needs of the organisation's customers. Her previous manager's style supported her high-level performance and her new manager was actively undermining it.

What about subtle below-the-line actions?

Jasmine's behaviour is quite obviously toxic, but what about more 'subtle' but similarly below-the line-behaviours?

As we reviewed earlier, Australian workplaces are legislated to be psychologically safe; bullying, discrimination and harassment are unlawful, yet rates are increasing not decreasing. The daily news is full of articles about the impact of below-the-line behaviours like bullying on social media, behaviours that shame and exclude colleagues, and the suicides caused by both subtle and overt psychological torture.

Although we are understandably very concerned about the prevalence of such unlawful behaviours, we also need to be aware of working to reduce the occurrence of the more subtle below-the-line behaviours. When behaviours like eye-rolling, excluding people, continual bitching and gossiping are acceptable, they create a festering psychological environment where the slide into a serious cesspool of toxicity easily occurs.

We make assumptions about acceptable workplace behaviour

Recently, a wise and experienced workforce advisor participated in a workplace program I was delivering. We were discussing how leaders operate above and below the line, and he shared that he had to be taught that eye-rolling was not appropriate conduct at work. For someone who seemed so kind and considerate of his employees, I was surprised yet grateful for his candour.

We would like to assume that we all know how to operate above the line. However, we have probably all been influenced by below-the-line behaviours in our homes, schools, communities and society by adults in our lives. We've possibly been on the receiving end of some that were very hurtful and even traumatising.

We may be unaware of the ingrained behaviours we have become accustomed to; regardless, they can be damaging and destructive to people and, ultimately, to organisational success. It can take a long time for us to unlearn certain patterns of behaviour and adopt new ways of interacting. In the meantime, however, below-the-line leaders can leave a massive wake of damage and trauma, let alone sabotage business outcomes, through undermining employees' performance and productivity.

Jasmine clearly lacks the above-the-line relationship skills of her predecessor Joe. She exhibits so many below-the-line behaviours. What do you think is going on for her?

- Does Jasmine lack leadership skills?
- Does she lack relationship skills?
- Is she so busy, overwhelmed and pressured that she stopped prioritising common decency in her leadership responsibilities?

- Is she actually experiencing burnout?
- Does she see high performers like Anna as a threat?
- Does she regularly use fear to intimidate people to gain control?
- Is she a bully, psychopath or narcissist?

It is impossible to know from the outside what is going on for Jasmine, but we can say that regardless of what causes this behaviour, it is definitively below the line.

Let's examine each of these possibilities to understand what might be influencing Jasmine's below-the-line behaviour.

A. Limited people leadership skills

Many people are promoted into leadership roles due to their professional or technical excellence. Although they have expertise, they may seriously lack the interpersonal skills of leadership. In fact, in many industries, the very skills required for professional excellence may be the antithesis of what research indicates is necessary for people leadership.[82,83]

Capabilities for professional / technical excellence	Capabilities for people leadership excellence
Known for what you know	Know that you don't know it all
Decisive	Open and curious
Need to be certain	Capacity to sit with uncertainty
Authoritative	Collaborative
Knowledgeable	Can model fallibility
Privilege thinking, logic, data, facts, figures, knowns	Privilege values, relationships, emotions, unknowns
Value judgement	Value non-judgement and acceptance
Mitigate risks	Value risks, for example, interpersonal risks of learning

Actively avoid weakness or vulnerability	Understand vulnerability = growth and learning
Reputation and credibility are cultivated	Authentic connection is cultivated

The challenge for many leaders is that they bring the very same capabilities necessary for technical excellence into their leadership roles. It is hard to switch from one modus operandi to another. It requires a high degree of self-awareness, and cognitive and psychological agility. As we have explored already, our capacity to operate with this level of agility comes from functioning from our executive brain.

One hypothesis may be that Jasmine is a technical expert and is lacking the capabilities in people leadership.

B. Limited relationship skills

Building above-the-line relationships with our direct reports requires us to build on our existing relationship skills.

We all have diverse relationship abilities depending on what our life experiences have taught us about interpersonal relationships. Some of us have learned that interpersonal relationships are generally safe and that, with some discernment, most people can be trusted.

If we had more negative experiences in relationships at home and / or at work, this may have dampened our capacity to trust others and may have taught us to live in self-protective mode. Tragically, some people in our society have experienced trauma or very difficult circumstances that have led them to build strong defences for self-preservation. This often results in a more protracted process of building trust in interpersonal relationships.

Arriving in adulthood, we assume that everyone has basic relationship skills, and yet, that is clearly not the case.

During childhood, the relationships we have with our primary caregivers create relationship templates that forge the way we are likely to approach relationships and interact with others in adulthood.

Research shows that these templates have common characteristics and are not just influential in how we develop personal relationships but in how they can drive our relationships at work.[84,85,86,87]

Only 60 per cent of the workforce emerges from childhood with a secure attachment style. A secure attachment style helps us trust others and ourselves, and makes navigating interpersonal relationships more straightforward. The other styles of attachment are:

1. Anxious and concerned with upsetting others. This is also known as people pleasing.
2. Dismissive and avoidant when we believe we're better than everyone else. This leads to not trusting and micromanaging.
3. Fearful and avoidant. This is when we are anxious but respond to this with avoidant behaviour such as becoming reserved and withdrawn.

If we were to use this as a lens to understand Jasmine's behaviour, her actions would be classified as *dismissive and avoidant, resulting in micromanaging.*

C. Overwhelmed and pressured

When people experience excessively high demands for the number of hours they work, they understandably look for ways to conserve mental and emotional energy. A common strategy is to become transactional in their way of functioning to diminish the energy required for interpersonal interactions.

It is possible that Jasmine has stopped prioritising basic human decency from her leadership responsibilities due to the level of overwhelm she is experiencing. We can probably all relate to attempting to minimise interactions with others as a way of conserving energy.

However, if this continues regularly, as it has in this situation, we fail to fulfil part of our leadership responsibilities.

D. Experiencing burnout

Is Jasmine experiencing burnout?

According to the WHO, burnout is a syndrome conceptualised as the result of chronic workplace stress that has not been successfully managed. It is specifically an occupational phenomenon and is characterised by three main factors:

- Feelings of energy depletion or exhaustion. This can be physical, mental or emotional.
- Increased mental distance from one's job. Feelings of negativism or cynicism related to one's job.
- Reduced professional efficacy.

If Jasmine is experiencing burnout, she may have nothing left to give her role, and her inability to be a leader to Anna may be due to this fact rather than her not having the requisite skills.

E. Feeling threatened

It is possible that Jasmine sees high performers like Anna as a threat.

Moving into a new workplace and establishing one's credibility can be challenging for anyone. Being new plus having a steep learning curve is not always an easy process. And having to do this in public as a leader, especially when you have direct reports who are extremely capable, can be triggering. Not everyone is comfortable with being a learner, especially when we are learning in public. This position can trigger uncomfortable emotions in us, which can be dealt with by projecting and blaming others.

It is possible that Jasmine shamed Anna because she feels ashamed of herself. This unconscious defence mechanism is called projection. Some people use this coping mechanism to deal with uncomfortable feelings by projecting them onto others. They make other people feel their uncomfortable feelings.

This type of behaviour is below the line and irresponsible, yet unfortunately it's incredibly common.

F. Terminally below the line: dangerous workplace operators— psychopaths and narcissists

A very tricky aspect of the contemporary workplace is the presence of psychopaths and narcissists. Although 5–10 per cent of the population may qualify as psychopathic, research shows that there may be an overrepresentation of psychopathic traits in corporate leaders—up to 21 per cent in some Australian organisations.[88,89]

Psychopaths and narcissists lack empathy. They are more focused on themselves and their own needs. This means they don't follow the common rules of interpersonal engagement where we make space to consider our own needs *and* the needs of others.

It is possible that Jasmine is a psychopath or high on narcissism. She lacks empathy and appears to have no capacity or desire to listen to Anna when she expresses her concerns. Her behaviour is clearly bullying.

When we are dealing with people who don't follow reasonable rules of interpersonal engagement, we need to be more self-protective. Our expectation will need to be adjusted and moderated. Although it would be helpful if psychopaths and narcissists were easily identifiable, it can be tricky to figure this out initially when working with someone. David Gillespie's book, *Taming Toxic People*, provides some insights into this.[90]

Working with a psychopath or narcissist can take a serious toll on your mental health. Psychopaths lack empathy. They are dishonest and manipulative; they are unwilling to take responsibility for their failings; and they are unwilling to learn from others—they only look out for themselves. Narcissists have some similar traits but are more self-absorbed, less aware and less intentionally manipulative. Narcissists seek admiration and attention; whereas, psychopaths are more exploitative and focused on their end goal.

Regardless of your leadership skill or behaviour, an employee who is psychopathic or narcissistic will only behave above the line if it serves them.

There is a substantial body of research as to the destructive impact of these personalities in the workplace and excellent resources exploring ways to self-protect from these toxic types.[91]

It is important to understand that the above-the-line approach works with the vast majority of the population who have the capacity and propensity to function above the line.

When an employee's modus operandi is far below the line, it shines a light on how necessary it is to include behavioural standards and skills of the workplace as part of the key performance criteria. Interestingly, in April 2020, Iceland passed legislation to prevent people with these personality types from holding public office.[92]

The question is open as to whether Jasmine regularly uses fear to intimidate people to gain control, and whether she is psychopathic or narcissistic.

What is influencing Jasmine's behaviour?

After reviewing these six areas, it is difficult to assess which one (or more) factors are at play. However, it is important to recognise that there may be multiple factors going on to contribute to this situation. Regardless, Jasmine's behaviour is below the line, and none of these factors make her behaviour acceptable or justified.

Positive relationships bring out the best in people

We understand that the quality of our relationships at work makes a substantial difference to productivity, performance and engagement. This highlights why the relationship we have with our direct line manager / leader is so pivotal to our functioning.

Recent advances in neuroscience show us that our highest cognitive functions occur in our executive brain. There are nine important executive brain functions that allow us to function at our peak cognitively and psychologically.

One of the most profound understandings from this research is the central role that relationships play in helping us access these brain functions. Positive relationships, where we feel understood and appreciated, help us function more fully from the executive brain.[93]

The emerging area of interpersonal neurobiology shows exactly what is occurring in the brain when we feel safe, understood and valued in relationships. Our reptile brain relaxes, and we have all of our cognitive and psychological (executive) functions available to dedicate to our work. We concentrate better and are more creative, strategic and lateral in our thinking. As we are less psychologically 'on guard', we are more open to others' perspectives, and we are more collaborative and less competitive. Our capacity for positive relationships with customers and colleagues is enhanced. Not surprisingly, we are more open to feedback and more willing to reflect on ways to improve our work performance and skills.

> *'It turns out that trust is in fact earned*
> *in the smallest of moments. It is earned*
> *not through heroic deeds, or even*
> *highly visible actions, but through*
> *paying attention, listening, and gestures*
> *of genuine care and connection.'*
> —Brené Brown

Investing in your employees

As the technological advances over recent years drive unprecedented change in organisations, employees are required to adapt to exceptional levels of change in their roles and respond rapidly to the ever-changing organisational context.

High-performing, agile and adaptable employees are extremely valuable to every business, workplace, leader and team at this time. Employees who are highly engaged bring their best selves to their roles. Driven to feel fulfilled from their work roles, they are committed and energised and bring their discretionary energy into their work.

Think about the amount of time, effort and energy your best performer requires?

In contrast, how much of your time, effort and energy does your most challenging employee require?

One way we can step into above-the-line leadership is to recognise and take responsibility to ensure that employees' core human needs can be met at work. All humans have a set of core needs that drive our behaviour. When these needs are met, we are provided with deep levels of wellbeing.

Core human needs

Given this, would it be reasonable to expect that our core human needs are considered and met by the workplace?

As mentioned in Chapter One, when these needs are not met at work, employees feel unsafe, disconnected and unfulfilled. They do not feel valued. Research has shown that this leads to a two-to three-fold increase in mental illness in the workforce.[94,95,96]

Making these needs more conscious is invaluable for everyone. It gives us each more control over directing our efforts in life to meet them. It also ensures a deeper understanding of ourselves and others. We often focus on differences as a way to make sense of the world around us.

In leadership development, we build a language of difference using a variety of frameworks. These frameworks can be invaluable but perhaps even more helpful when they are supported by appreciating the similarities and shared needs that all humans have.

As we outlined in Chapter One, our common and shared human needs are:

1. The need for safety: both physical and psychological.
2. The need for feeling valued: to recognise our inherent value—that we are capable of making worthwhile contributions and that we matter.
3. The need for fulfilment: to have meaning and purpose, to develop ourselves, to have opportunities to learn, grow and develop and to benefit from meaningful activities and from fun and satisfaction.
4. The need for connection: or a sense of belonging to groups that are important to us, like our workplace or team.

When our employees feel that these core human needs can be met through work, they are far more likely to have high-level commitment and engagement in their roles. This is especially important when the workplace benefits from people bringing their 'whole selves' to work.

Questions for reflection:

Think about the times when you were the most engaged in your professional role?

Which of these needs were being met?

Let's consider how these needs may show up in an above-the-line relationship with our employees.

a) Our need for **safety**

We have a need for both physical and psychological safety. What will be helpful in fostering psychological safety will be different for each person, but we know that there are some common themes. When we feel safe, our nervous system relaxes significantly at every level. The research on psychological safety clearly shows the impact it has on teamwork, performance and openness to learning.[97,98,99]

We don't feel psychologically safe when we are under continual siege from a negative and critical leader or from a leader who uses fear as a motivating tool. It places our nervous system in continual flight or fight mode.

Above-the-line leadership ensures employees feel physically and psychologically safe.

b) Our need for feeling **valued**

Everyone has a need to feel valued, worthy and that they matter. In the workplace, paying employees a salary is not enough to convey this message. People need to feel recognised for their contributions and efforts by those they work with and, in particular, by their direct line manager. When people feel valued they are likely to be more engaged and to bring discretionary effort into their roles.[100,101]

Above-the-line leadership ensures employees feel they are valued.

c) Our need for **fulfilment**

An essential motivator for us at work is to find fulfilment. We are encouraged from an early age to seek a career that aligns with our strengths, skills and values. One of the key ways we can lead above the line is to keep our employees' motivators in mind. We have the ability to tweak their roles and responsibilities to help them play to their strengths and achieve greater fulfilment in their work role.

What do you believe your employees need in order to be fulfilled? Dan Pink delivered a wonderful TED talk about what motivates us at work.[102] Watching it with employees can be a great prompter for a discussion about fulfilment through work. It helps build communication and openness and assists you in guiding them to play to their strengths and natural drivers.

Above-the-line leadership finds ways to support employees to achieve fulfilment in their professional roles and to benefit from the playfulness and fun that can be generated when people work well together.

d) Our need for **belonging** and **connection**

Human beings are wired to connect. Whether we are aware of it or not, when we feel isolated and disconnected, we release the stress hormones cortisol and adrenaline. This shows that disconnection makes us feel unsafe. Leading above the line involves a positive relationship with our employees. We don't have to be best friends or have an out-of-work relationship with them. Regardless of how we feel about our employees, we need to build a positive and constructive relationship that provides a sense of belonging and connection. Their relationship with you will be a primary factor in influencing their attitude towards the workplace and fulfilling their role. In this way, above-the-line leadership facilitates your employees' commitment to your workplace. In Chapter Seven, we will explore this at a team level.

During the current shutdown period of COVID-19, one of the greatest costs of remote working is the isolation and disconnection many people feel. Even the etiquette over screens, such as turning off cameras during zoom sessions and chat function usage, has become a powerful indicator of how willing or unwilling we are to connect with others.

Why do workplaces need above-the-line leadership?

The workplace needs the best our employees have to offer, so leaders need the collegial relationships and skills to facilitate expression of their employees' potential. Employee engagement can be improved in many workplaces. If employees don't feel valued by the workplace, they are likely to respond with disengagement. Research shows that employees who are disengaged or actively disengaged represent the bulk of the Australian workforce.[103]

Our connections give us protective factors that serve us well. This is especially important when we are under stress. Positive relationships actually help us regulate our neurophysiology. This means that when we have good connections with those whom we spend a lot of time, our body's nervous system has a greater capacity to cope with stress and pressure. So, the more stress we are under, the more we need good support and relationships.

If our workplace requires our employees to deal with a lot of stress, uncertainty, change, interpersonal strain or emotional wear and tear, above-the-line leadership would direct our focus to strengthen the relationships with our employees, thus providing them with a strong protective factor. This has been vital during this pandemic period.

IN SUMMARY

In this chapter, we reflected on the vital role of an employees' relationship with their direct line manager, and how this is a central factor in each employee's experience of their workplace. We also explored the dynamics at play when leaders lead below the line; how this can impact performance and productivity; and how toxic this can be on employees' wellbeing.

In Chapter Six, we'll explore ways to enrich the one-on-one relationships line managers have with their direct reports.

Questions for reflection:

What are the benefits of your employees functioning above the line?

What are the workplace behaviours that help your colleagues perform well?

What are the workplace behaviours that hinder your colleagues' ability to perform well?

Reflect back to these two questions posed in this chapter:

Think about the amount of time, effort and energy your best performer requires?

In contrast, how much of your time, effort and energy does your most challenging employee require?

How much easier does it make your role having better performing employees?

How much more time do you have available for real leadership and innovation, and for your own peak performance when you have a team of high performers?

Chapter Six

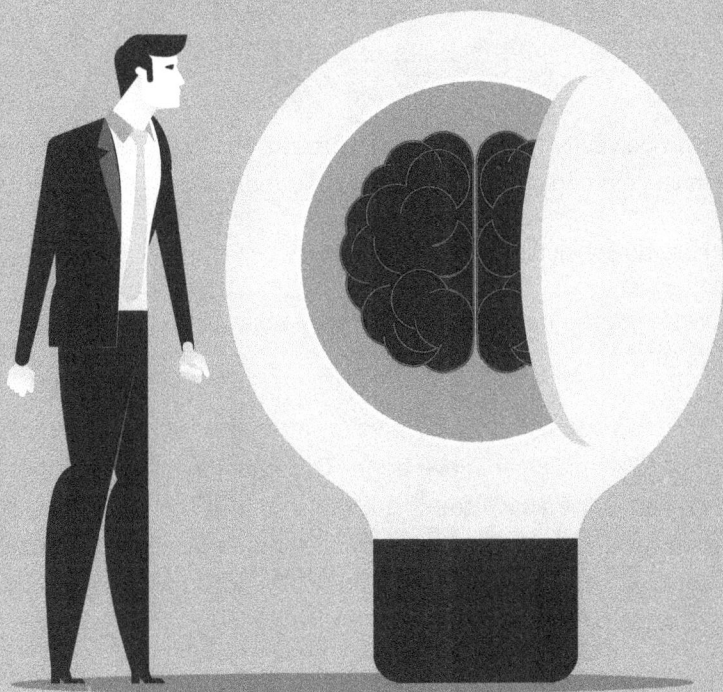

HOW TO LEAD EMPLOYEES ABOVE THE LINE

*'Every morning, you have a choice.
You can strive to lift people up or cut
them down. Don't fall for the worst
impulses in others. Rise to the occasion
and bring out the best in others.'*
—Adam Grant

How do you bring out the best in others? This must be one of the most common challenges that leaders today face.

How do you achieve this now?

What are the guiding principles that work for you and for your people?

Ensuring your employees function at their peak would be any organisation's competitive edge. This chapter will explore how we can utilise above-the-line leadership relationships and skills to maximise employees' performance and wellbeing, and address some of the trickier interpersonal challenges of contemporary leadership relationships.

Are you genuinely committed to helping employees thrive?

In the same way that strategic leadership advances the possibilities for an organisation, above-the-line leadership optimises the potential of each employee and their team. Great leaders have a well-developed capacity to see the possibilities for expansion, growth and development.

Our role as above-the-line leaders is not just about viewing employees as they're functioning now, it's about seeing their capabilities, guiding them to step into their potential and supporting their ongoing development.

When delivering people leadership development programs, I invite participants to articulate the common types of skills, qualities and talents of an ideal leader. This experience has shown that we value extremely similar qualities in our leaders. We recognise that regardless of our differences, there are common people leadership skills and qualities that are not just desirable but are hugely impactful in the experience we all want to have at work.

These skills and qualities all point in the same direction. They are all necessary for trust, respect, cooperation, flexibility, responsibility, hard work and growth to prevail. They also provide us with guidance about how we prefer to establish and participate in workplace relationships.

In Chapter Three, I invited you to identify your own preferences regarding the attributes of a good leader and contrast this with your own self-leadership style.

Now, let's review the following table in terms of how you lead others.

How do you lead others?

Sometimes our intentions are to lead above the line, but in reality our behaviours are below the line.

Qualities of leadership	
Disrespectful	Respectful
Defensive	Accountable
Unnecessarily critical	Committed to your learning and growth
Unreliable	Reliable
Blaming	Principled
Egocentric	Self-aware
Impatient	Consistent
Untrustworthy	Trustworthy
Manipulative	Appreciative
Harshly judgemental	Supportive
Micromanaging	Empowered
Bullying	Courageous
Mean-spirited	Generous
Controlling	Easygoing
Below-the-line leadership	Above-the-line leadership

How do you believe your employees experience your leadership?

If you were to use the table above as a 360° tool, what results would you get?

What would your direct reports see as your strengths and general approach?

What would they perceive as learning opportunities for you?

If they expressed one area as the biggest priority for your learning, what would it be?

As we have reflected on a lot in this book, above-the-line leadership involves a significant skill set that starts from within. This includes:

1. Self-awareness: being able and willing to know and understand your own strengths, weakness and learning edges.

2. Accountability: being comfortable taking personal responsibility and managing boundaries and self-care.

3. Self-direction and self-leadership: leading yourself with your values, taking responsibility for your own core human needs, and bringing out the best in yourself.

4. Self-management: manage your own ego, mood, energy and triggers.

5. Interpersonal flexibility: the ability to adapt your communication skills and style to different situations with different people and dynamics.

Barriers to leading above the line

Let's review some common inner barriers that may undermine our capacity to build these skills and lead others above the line.

1. Lack of self-trust

> *The relationships we have with the*
> *world are largely determined by the*
> *relationships we have with ourselves.'*
> — Greg Anderson

A common barrier to building a positive relationship with employees is trust. Our capacity to build trusting relationships depends on the degree to which we have learned to trust ourselves.

If we lack trust in ourselves, we'll find it hard to trust others. This will often result in more below-the-line behaviours such as controlling or micromanaging.

Trust builds psychological safety.

Are you a micromanager?

Most leaders are unaware when they lapse into micromanagement and the below-the-line dynamic that this creates.

Do any of the following describe you?

You often think you'll do it yourself because you will do it right or better.

You're not confident in your employees. This justifies your need to spend time monitoring their approach, their progress and the details.

You often feel your employees could have done a better job and you focus on the small details that could be improved, rather than the large proportion that was completed successfully.

Your employees ask very few questions of you and don't seek guidance from you.

The more you ask your employees about their work, the more they cover up and hide their work from you.

When employees do not achieve well, you see problems, and you are unaware of the opportunities for growth and development for which they need your guidance.

Micromanagement is below the line

We need to give employees space to build skills, capabilities and confidence. Micromanaging is a short-term solution to the long-term challenge of building trust, autonomy and high-performing skills. It undermines morale, productivity and the long-term peak performance you are striving to achieve.

Micromanagement is based on old-style command-and-control principles. No-one likes to be micromanaged, yet it is still too common in the workplace. It's an awful experience for employees and creates the opposite of what the behaviour is trying to address.

2. Automatic judgement

If we're very self-critical, we're likely to be very critical of others. If we're toxic towards ourselves (shaming, blaming, negating, bullying and undermining), this may be reflected in how we relate to others. As previously acknowledged, if we are high on empathy, we are less likely to be continually critical of others, but if we are lower on empathy then automatic judgement may be our modus operandi.

If our reptile brain dominates, the habit of judging others and seeing others in limited ways may dominate: being nit-picky or criticising and fixating on weaknesses instead of seeing undeveloped skills as opportunities for learning.

We need to lift our own self-leadership above the line for the benefit of our own productivity and performance, for the maximisation of our untapped potential, and so that we are able to lead others well.

> *'Whenever you are about to find fault with someone, ask yourself the following question: What fault of mine most nearly resembles the one I'm about to criticize?'*
> —Marcus Aurelius

Questions for reflection:

Has your inner critical voice become an outer weapon of mass destruction?

What do you tend to notice in others? Their strengths or weaknesses?

How much positive feedback are you aware you give to others?

How much constructive critical feedback are you aware you give to others?

What would your ratio of positive feedback to constructive critical feedback look like?

3. Our ego and triggers

As a teenager of the 70s, I listened to a famous Australian band called Skyhooks who wrote a song called *Ego is not a dirty word*. It was the hit single from their No 1 album also called *Ego is not a dirty word*. It was the first song I'd ever heard that talked about our inner workings beyond love, loss and heartache.

What it acknowledged was that our ego has a helpful role to play and that it can help us appreciate who we are and our unique talents, gifts and potential contributions.

The problem with the ego is when it dominates to the detriment of everyone else. It is the drain in the ecosystem that absorbs all the best nutrients and leaves other living elements to starve.

If our ego is fragile or insecure, a huge amount of our energy can be consumed trying to buoy it or trying to feed off others. Fragile or insecure egos are a cause of many toxic behaviours that create immense dysfunction in the workplace.

Toxic leadership is below the line

Toxic leadership serves the dysfunctional aspects of the leader, not the organisation or the employees they are there to support.

It involves a combination of self-oriented attitudes, motivations and behaviours that have adverse effects on employees, the organisation and its performance. Toxic leaders are self-serving and preoccupied with their own agendas; they lack concern for the wellbeing of others. Toxic leaders often deny the negative impact of their behaviour on the life force of the workplace.

Toxic leadership arises when leaders operate in psychologically irresponsible ways. They function in what we would describe as a 'psychologically primitive' way, and they easily become locked in a cycle of stress, blame and conflict. Bullying and damaging interpersonal interactions can follow, which creates a massive cost to the workforce and culture.

How can we straighten above-the-line leadership?

It starts with a mindset—an attitude or approach to others.

Stop employing brilliant jerks

Most workplaces employ people based on their professional or technical skills. We employ people for **what they do**. Our position descriptions are full of the professional and technical skills that people require to do the job. We prioritise candidates with technical and professional excellence and commonly gauge their style and personality type through the 'feel' of the interview and their responses to a few tired HR questions.

Unfortunately, this means we can unwittingly employ people who may be great at the professional or technical skills yet operate (in the workplace) in ways that are damaging to the performance and productivity of others.

Increasingly, the research highlights that how we approach our roles, how we show up at work, how emotionally intelligent we are, how we participate in teamwork and our openness to learning are as critical as the technical / professional skills required.[104]

If someone is poor in *how* they perform their role skills, they will be difficult to work with and hard to develop. They will not adapt well to change, and in an environment where teamwork is critical, their behaviours are likely to negatively impact the performance, productivity and engagement of others. Employees who are low on these skills will compromise a team's ability to get the job done well. Their behaviours are likely to be below the line and will negatively influence the people with whom they interact and work closely.

Many workplaces address this by identifying the workplace values that are seen as desirable. The challenge with this is complex. This notion assumes that by identifying the values, we'll have the necessary skills to align our behaviours with those values. It also assumes we can align our behaviours with those values when we are under immense stress and pressure; it works on the assumption that leaders and managers know how to enforce these values when employees operate outside of these. If these skills and values are not given a high priority on position descriptions (or KPIs), it is hard to performance-manage them.

We need to go beyond interviewing about values if we want to focus on the critical skills necessary to participate well in the workplace.

We can't make assumptions that people have these skills. At worst, people can be technically brilliant but interpersonally toxic. They can work against everything the company has worked towards. These **brilliant jerks** can be a disaster for your workplace and for the performance of your team.

Employ staff who are emotionally intelligent and open to learning

Employing staff who are emotionally intelligent has been increasingly accepted since the importance of EI skyrocketed over the past two decades. Research shows that EI skills are essential for workplace success.[105] EI is necessary for sustainable performance, productivity, and workplace wellbeing and culture, and includes self-awareness and self-management skills, and interpersonal relationship and teamwork skills.

Employing staff who are open to learning is vital. Workplaces and employees must continually adjust to unprecedented levels of change, innovation and technological advancement.

The capacity to be open to learning is critical for organisations and employees to keep up with the accelerating pace of change. No longer can employees function and approach their roles with the same skills from even five years ago. The need for change and adaptation was unparalleled, due to advances in technology, even before the current pandemic. It has skyrocketed since.

Everything is evolving so quickly and it is not just about being open to learning; it is about being cognitively and psychologically agile enough to keep up with the accelerated pace of change and having the ability to pivot constantly.

Some tips for recognising when people have skills in EI, teamwork skills and openness to learning:

- They take responsibility for themselves and don't use blaming language or pass the buck onto others.
- They are able to recognise their weaknesses and acknowledge areas for learning, growth and development.

- They have emotional literacy; they use language that includes emotions and the psychology of interpersonal relationships. Emotional literacy helps enormously with self-awareness and self-management.

Here are five steps you can take for prioritising EI, teamwork skills and an openness to learning:

1. Identify what EI, teamwork and openness to learning skills are necessary for the best functioning in:
   a) your workplace
   b) your team
   c) the specific role

2. Include EI, teamwork and openness to learning on position descriptions—specify the skills necessary for the role, for the teamwork required and for contributing to the values and desired culture of the workplace. If the skills have been articulated in the position description, you can address them as workplace skills necessary for the position.

3. Interview potential employees based on EI, teamwork and the openness to learning skills most relevant to your workplace. Ask questions that can help illuminate someone's capabilities in these areas.

4. Give positive feedback when employees use EI, teamwork and openness to learning skills. If you provide specific feedback when your employees use these highly valued skills, they will use them more often and in broader contexts. Give positive feedback in private and public arenas.

5. Address the behaviours and skills when a lack of EI, teamwork and openness to learning is evident. One of the biggest challenges is having the confidence and

commitment to have the tricky conversations as needed. (We'll explore this in more detail later in this chapter.)

Build positive relationships

'A brave leader is someone who says
I see you. I hear you. I don't have all
the answers, but I'm going to keep
listening and asking questions.'

—Brené Brown

A positive relationship is an incredibly powerful force in a workplace environment. Research shows that a positive relationship with our direct line manager is a protective factor when we are under stress.[106] It helps meet our core human needs, helps us perform at our peak and supports our wellbeing.

Positive regard for others involves bringing positive intent and assuming the best in people. This works well for the bulk of the population, except when people are narcissistic or psychopathic. If you are managing a psychopath or narcissist, the guiding principles of this chapter do not apply. These guiding principles only apply to people who are capable of building healthy above-the-line workplace relationships.

When leaders genuinely bring positive regard to relationships with their employees, it is a powerful force to bridge connection. Genuine interest in how others see the world breeds trust and psychological safety.

'You don't change culture through
emails and memos. You change
it through relationships ... one
conversation at a time.'

—Danny Steele

Set a positive tone

How do you set the tone for your workplace relationships? What vibe do you bring?

Above-the-line leaders set an optimistic and appreciative tone. The fact they encourage and value their people is evident in their day-to-day interactions. It is obvious in their greetings, presence and vibe.

Pay attention—be present—hold space

What are you paying attention to? When in the presence of your direct reports, what are you focused on? How do you show up and be present?

Can you reflect on your direct reports without it being about you? Do you know what is important to them? What do you remember about their priorities?

Be a good active listener

How do you listen? Are you an active listener? Do you listen to understand or listen to reply?

Can you listen with a neutral positive lens or do you tend to come from a place of negative judgement? Do you ask open-ended questions to help you understand more of what your direct report is saying?

Be a supportive influence

Positively influence the way employees are engaged at work through problem-solving, feedback, and valuing and being supportive of others. A positive working environment supports us to effectively manage issues that affect performance.

Appreciation

> 'Great leaders don't influence you to be
> like them; they inspire you to be yourself.'
> —Alexander den Heijer

Develop positive awareness and understanding of each individual. Understand their strengths and give positive feedback about skills and strengths.

Express gratitude and keep employees 'in mind'.

Aim to understand

One of the most powerful ways to build rapport with our employees is to know and understand what makes them tick, and when and how their core human needs are being met in the workplace environment.

> 'Leadership is about making others better
> as a result of your presence and making
> sure that impact lasts in your absence.'
> —Sheryl Sandberg

When you understand your employees' core needs at work, it helps you understand their motivations. In the workplace, employees will function at their peak if their core human needs are being met.

Value their strengths

'You hired them for their strengths.
Why focus on their weaknesses?'
—Ahmed Karam

No fault found

I know an electronic technician with a strong inclination for noticing the negative and commenting on it. Like many of our roles, his job is always to be on alert for, find, analyse and fix faults. His long career in his industry has unintentionally wired his brain to be a fault seeking machine.

Think about how this must affect him and his life. His brain is wired to continuously notice and find faults. I'm guessing you have realised this is not good for one's mental health.

In his industry, if there is no fault, the item is labelled NO FAULT FOUND. There is no language to even say working well, or even working. It is just NO FAULT FOUND.

Research shows that most of us are like my electronic technician friend. We have a negativity bias; we look for and notice the negatives far more than the positives.[107,108] We mainly notice faults and if there are no faults, we tend to have little on which to comment. We may notice the positives but have not prioritised putting these into words. If no fault is found, we quickly move on to the next task.

Leaders and managers often inadvertently lead below the line with a tendency to fixate and focus on the negative. They tend to give far more specific feedback about weaknesses than about strengths. They tend to ignore a lot of the positive skills and strengths that people have. And if they do notice them, they don't articulate them out loud; they don't put them into words; they don't give that positive and affirming feedback.

When employees have opportunities for growth and learning, leaders tend to give more critical and detailed feedback rather than looking to guide in skill development. At the same time, when it comes to positives, they tend to give more feedback about effort and outcomes than on skills and strengths. Feedback about effort has its positives; it encourages and values the efforts employees contribute, yet in a commercial environment, where most employees have more work than they can complete in their working hours, feedback about effort can feel futile. Where can you go with that?

Regarding outcomes, we are not often 100 per cent in control of outcomes. Of course, this will vary between organisations and industries, but in many environments, there are factors outside of employees' control in achieving the desired outcomes.

Specific skill- and strength-based positive feedback is far more impactful as a counterbalance to specific feedback about weaknesses and learning opportunities. It also complements the 'effort and outcome' feedback by providing a richer appreciation of the value of employees' contributions.

'Leaders don't look for recognition from others; they look for others to recognise.'
—Simon Sinek

The power of positive feedback

Research will show that the more you give employees specific feedback about their skills and strengths, the more they will intentionally use them.

There is an outdated and mistaken perception that if we give people positive feedback about their strengths and skills, they'll get cocky and sit on their laurels. But in fact, research shows the opposite. When employees know specifically how their skills, strengths, knowledge and efforts are valued and appreciated, they are likely to work harder and contribute their wisdom and skills more confidently.[109]

Interestingly, when employees know how they are perceived in terms of their skills and strengths, they are more likely to ask for guidance when they are uncertain. They are more likely to ask for and welcome constructive feedback, and question organisational direction when it doesn't seem right.

Are you actually giving people feedback about their skills and strengths? Or when you give positive feedback, are you predominantly, like most people, giving feedback primarily about their effort and the outcome?

*'True leadership stems from individuality
that is honestly and sometimes
imperfectly expressed .... Leaders should
strive for authenticity over perfection.'*
—Sheryl Sandberg

Providing unbalanced feedback to our colleagues is another way of leading below the line. In terms of workplace relationships and team environments, research shows we need, roughly, five positives to every one negative for the relationship to be healthy.[110,111] This ratio extends from professional to personal relationships—from teamwork to the intimacy of a couple's relationship.

When I say this in a training or mentoring session, people often baulk at me and ask, *how could I possibly find five positives to every one negative?* It's actually quite easy but may take some practice (as long as we're not dealing with a narcissist or psychopath). The truth is that unless someone is destructive in a work environment, there is a lot more to say that's positive about people.

The barrier is that we are not in the habit of recognising or acknowledging positives. We don't even appreciate what there is, and hence, we don't have a language for them. This is especially so if we're self-critical. Now, if this is the case for you, if you've been self-critical, you may have fewer words to describe strengths and more to describe weaknesses and limitations.

And yes, of course, all of those weaknesses are developmental opportunities so they can be very helpful. It's useful to give people feedback and help them elevate performance and build skills in a positive way. That's essential for building a successful, innovative and high-performing team.

Strengths awareness and amplification

- Can you recognise and write a list of ten of the finest skills and ten of the top strengths of your key team members?

- What's quicker? Writing a list of ten weaknesses or writing a list of ten strengths of each of your team members?

- How do you put effort into valuing and appreciating your team members? How do you help your team members learn and develop their skills and abilities?

Help them learn and develop

> *'You don't inspire people by showing how powerful you are; you inspire people by showing how powerful they are.'*
>
> —Alexander den Heijer

One of the most powerful ways to engage above-the-line leadership is to support the learning and growth of employees. Helping people be at their best is an empowering gift.

If your leader creates an environment or provides you with skills and guidance to be the best you can be, how does that impact you?

Workplaces often take a pedestrian approach to professional development. They provide a course or a workshop to 'tick the box' and think the training is done.

A common approach to workplace learning and professional development is to focus on fixing weaknesses. As we just described, research shows that employees tend to get detailed feedback about weaknesses while ignoring skills and strengths.[112] We need to build a mindset focused on growth and development.

When things do not go the way we had hoped, rather than playing the blame game, we need to ask:

- How is this a learning opportunity?
- What skills or knowledge can we develop to increase performance in this situation?

This helps to build psychological safety.

When the workplace is a psychologically safe learning culture, with a strong commitment to lifelong learning, your employees:

- own their learning needs and are self-directed, lifelong learners
- appreciate and build on their skills and strengths
- seek out feedback for improvement
- grow, develop and become agile as needed by the ever-changing world in which we live.

In a psychologically safe workplace, employees are relaxed. Their egos aren't an obstacle to professional development. This above-the-line environment ensures there are no interpersonal risks to learning in the workplace. Employees feel safe to ask questions to indicate when they are uncertain, to seek guidance openly, and to value the ongoing process of masterful development.

'Don't discount the power of your
words. The thought that they might
cause unnecessary hurt or discomfort
should inform every conversation.'
—P M Forni

Above-the-line communication involves respect, appreciation, kindness and dignity of the other person and you. All messages, feedback or learning that needs to be conveyed must be separated out from the way we treat our employees.

People listen to feedback when they feel heard and when we approach them with empathy and respect.

Positively manage tricky conversations

Having tricky conversations can be one of the more challenging aspects of any interpersonal relationship, let alone in leadership.

Giving and receiving feedback is a complex interaction. Unfortunately, we've probably all been on the receiving end of below-the-line feedback, where the aim was to put us down so the other person could feel better about themselves.

Above-the-line feedback assists our employees to be the best they can be. The key goal of feedback is to assist employees to function better from a genuine desire to support them to flourish. Other goals of feedback are to inform employees of information or knowledge, to bring their attention to skills that need development, and to redirect focus when perspective or priorities are lost. Feedback helps to sharpen their focus.

Giving feedback from an above-the-line perspective demonstrates true commitment to employees' development.

Strategies for having above-the-line tricky conversations

Before you give feedback to your employees, work to understand their preferences regarding being on the receiving end of feedback. We all have preferences regarding feedback, although we may not be able to articulate them readily. Ask your employee how they like getting feedback. If they don't have an answer, ask them to recount a time when receiving feedback was a positive experience.

Feedback forces us to deal with the fact that we need to learn and grow.

The classic approach to giving feedback is the shit sandwich of providing negative feedback between two positives. The issue here is that it feels staged and untrue. We all have a strong bullshit radar, so the shit sandwich feels fake and forced. However, the underlying intention behind this classic approach to feedback is sound: we need to give more positive feedback than negative.

Meet Mario

Mario is a leader who participated in a leadership development program I delivered at his workplace.

He was faced with having a difficult conversation with Abhi, one of his direct reports whom he had been very tolerant with and extremely supportive of over the two years previous. He had to give Abhi constructive criticism about the angry and inappropriate emails he would send when he was frustrated with his work (not with Mario personally).

He started by congratulating Abhi on a compliment he received about his work. Abhi was aware that he had informed the team about the compliment, which he had consented to. He then praised him for his commitment to his work role.

He empathised with Abhi's frustrations and realised that he was displacing his anger on other people. He explained to Abhi the expectations of behaviour at work: professionalism and respect for one another, regardless of individual roles.

Mario asked him how he could help and his response was that he was already being supportive. Abhi apologised for his behaviour and said that he was working on it. Mario requested him to be mindful of the tone of his emails and ensure they were respectful. Mario encouraged him to be open to constructive feedback that comes from a good place. Mario's feedback was aimed at helping Abhi improve his skills and work performance. Mario asked if he was being unreasonable with his request and Abhi said he was not.

Mario's reflections

'While it is hard to find positive things about people when the obvious negative characteristics show up, I realise that I need to try harder. I owe it to people to give them every opportunity to redeem themselves and for me to still see the good in them, no matter what—no excuses. I will strive to find five good things for one bad trait.'

What did Mario do well?

He was kind, respectful and empathetic.

He prioritised positive relationships.

He prepared for the conversation in terms of the key points (but also emotionally).

He set a positive tone.

Mario was centred and calm, so he was far less likely to be reactive if his direct report did not respond well.

He set a positive tone, paid attention and was fully present.

He reminded himself and his direct report of his strengths.

He valued his strengths and the power of positive feedback.

He approached his direct report's behaviour as a learning opportunity.

He looked for the opportunity for growth and learning.

He was clear.

He brought clarity and appreciation to the conversation.

He empathised with the frustrations that may have contributed to his direct report's behaviour.

His aim was to understand.

He asked how he could be helpful.

He sought to be a positive, supportive influence.

He brought no agendas to put his direct report down.

He navigated a tricky conversation in respectful and psychologically safe ways.

He was above the line.

'I always bring my core values to feedback conversations. I specifically bring courage, which means that I don't choose comfort over being respectful and honest—choosing politeness over respect is not respectful.'

—Brené Brown

When employees function below the line

So, you might be left wondering what happens when your direct report is functioning below the line?

It is difficult to manage someone who consistently functions poorly at an interpersonal level. We understand, however, that we may each occasionally dip below the line in moments of high stress and that we need to take responsibility for those times. Mario's direct report, Abhi, was operating below the line occasionally. He lacked self-awareness and self-management skills, and Mario brought this to his attention in the respectful conversation just outlined.

Mario shared that prior to his experience with Abhi, he had tolerated a below-the-line direct report over a long period with significant consequences. Mario regretted that he never addressed this situation directly. He kept hoping things would improve. He didn't want to make things worse by having a conversation with which he felt ill equipped to deal. This situation had a terrible impact on Mario's team; all of his peak performers left as they found the below-the-line behaviours of one employee intolerable.

It is challenging when people function below the line every day at work, and not all workplaces have the skills and systems in place to deal with this well. What happens in your workplace?

As discussed in the last two chapters, we want to stop employing brilliant jerks—or jerks altogether. However, when someone is very often operating below the line, we need to address this directly. We need to find the best ways to identify the minimum standards of acceptable interpersonal behaviour and ensure that employees have opportunities to develop the interpersonal and self-management skills required to participate productively in the psychological environment.

You may not even be aware of someone functioning below the line interpersonally, as they may be a master at keeping it hidden and demonstrating their best behaviour in your presence.

Questions for reflection:

Does the employee who functions below the line have the required interpersonal skills?

If not, what can be done to support them to develop these skills?

If yes, what is occurring for this employee not to be using these skills? Is it situational?

How do you recognise and encourage above-the-line behaviours?

IN SUMMARY

In this chapter, we reflected on how to employ the right people, and how to build positive, strength-based relationships that support learning and development. Navigating tricky conversations and providing engaging and motivating feedback are essential parts of the toolkit for supporting an above-the-line workplace.

In Chapter Seven, we'll turn our attention towards the team as a whole, reflecting on the complexity of interpersonal dynamics in a team setting.

Questions for reflection:

When do your employees feel valued?

When do your employees feel connected?

When do your employees feel fulfilled?

When do your employees feel unsafe?

When do your employees feel devalued?

When do your employees feel disconnected?

When do your employees feel unfulfilled?

If your leader / manager asked you these questions and then used your answers to influence their relationship with you, how would that land for you?

Chapter Seven

ARE YOU LEADING A
THRIVING ECOSYSTEM OR
A TOXIC EGO-SYSTEM?

*'Organizational culture is the 'water'
in the fishbowl. If the water is clean,
nourishing, energising, the fish will thrive
and if the water is toxic the fish will die
leaving the infrastructure value-less.'*
—Ranjan De Silva

The natural world teaches us about thriving and good health. Thriving ecosystems are healthy for all living things within an interconnected environment. If in balance, an ecosystem sustains the health of everything within it; it is well-supported by the natural flow of nutrition, growth and energy. While an overload of toxins can be tolerated in the short term, eventually, the natural balance will break down and the toxins will negatively affect the whole.

Leading a healthy team and workplace

The psychological environment or ecosystem your people are marinating in each day has a huge and powerful impact on them at every level.

In a thriving ecosystem where employees feel valued, teams perform at their peak cognitively and psychologically. The impact can be exceptionally positive as it unleashes the potential of the workforce—it is primed to think and perform at its peak. This environment, like any flourishing ecosystem, supports and sustains individuals in cohesive ways, and naturally fosters productive collaboration and teamwork.

A toxic 'ego-system', where people feel unsafe and unvalued, and where toxic interpersonal interactions are rife, reinforces reptile brain functioning that undermines all workplace aspirations, performances and values.

Workplaces are complex ecosystems

Everyone benefits when the workplace ecosystem functions from an abundance of factors (nutrients) that foster growth, balance and regulation. An organisation's capacity to achieve its goals and the employees' needs for fulfilment and wellbeing are best served by a healthy ecosystem.

Workplace ecosystems influence performance, productivity, health and wellbeing, and include the physical, psychological and interpersonal environment in which employees are immersed each day. It is harder for employees to work and be productive in a poor workplace ecosystem. Eventually, the toxin build-up is so destructive, it can threaten the organisation's very survival.

Workplace ecosystems can be cultivated to improve performance

Traditional approaches used to improve productivity and performance have had an individualistic rather than systemic or interpersonal focus. They often fail to address the impact that interpersonal dynamics and workplace behaviours have on achieving organisational goals and meeting KPIs. When employees underperform, the focus tends to locate the problem in the individual. It doesn't consider the many other contributing factors.

Individually focused approaches concentrate on what employees **do**. They neglect **how** employees work together and **how** their interactions create an environment that either drives or undermines performance.

Above-the-line teamwork

Leading a team above the line shifts our focus to positively influence interpersonal interactions between team members so we can build cohesion and psychological safety that optimises everyone's performance and engagement. This is no easy feat. Yet, the research states that this is the best way to achieve an organisation's goals.

The hard part is that interpersonal behaviours and dynamics are complex and ever-changing.

The challenges of above-the-line teamwork

Working closely in teams does not always bring out the best in people. Petty jealousies, rivalries, gossiping, bitchiness, competitiveness, unnecessary criticism or lack of cooperation can easily take hold if we don't harness and positively influence the interpersonal environment and team dynamics.

Let's face it, we spend a lot of time with our colleagues. Well, we certainly did prior to the current pandemic. We have generally spent more time with our colleagues than we have spent with our loved ones. Fulfilling our work roles can require a lot of interaction, cooperation and interdependency, especially while under pressure and stress. This can bring up patterns of behaviour and dynamics that can negatively impact the ecosystem. We are not all tuned in to the interplay of interpersonal dynamics; therefore, we may be unaware of the undercurrents affecting team performance and productivity. These are even harder to recognise and influence when we're working remotely.

Our individual impact on the ecosystem

While growing up, we each develop a set of coping mechanisms that help us deal with pressure and stress. Some of these are adaptive and some are maladaptive. As we mature and build life wisdom, we generally evolve and develop more adaptive ways of handling difficult things.

When under pressure, we can easily revert to our less mature ways of coping. Our most petty selves pop up in our behaviour before we've had a moment to think about how we should respond. The more toxic or below the line the environment is, the more likely we'll shift gears into self-protection. This only encourages that reptile brain to kick in again and amplify our maladaptive behaviours less driven by cooperation and collaboration.

A thriving ecosystem, where employees feel psychologically safe, valued and open to learning, increases the likelihood that people will support each other to perform at their peak. This environment, like any flourishing ecosystem, supports and sustains individuals in cohesive ways, naturally fostering productive collaboration and teamwork. It also becomes a positive virtuous cycle, building goodwill and sustainability.

What impact does a thriving workplace ecosystem have?

When most parts of a workplace ecosystem are healthy and positive, it replenishes and nurtures. Good energy is created collectively. Even just walking into the office in the morning can be uplifting when you are greeted by colleagues who care about you and who appreciate your unique skills and strengths. A thriving ecosystem creates an environment where everyone's positive performance synergistically amplifies the performance of others. The study of this is interpersonal or social neurobiology.[113]

The whole is greater than the sum of the parts

What this ultimately means is that the team contributes more *collectively* than it would *individually*. When you add up the individual contributions of each team member, you will see what an above-the-line team is capable of. This amplification results from everyone who is part of that team. We see this work well on the footy field, in a theatre and in an orchestra. It is not surprising that the focus of performance psychologists for sports teams is not just on the individual performance but on the interpersonal dynamics of the team. The 2019 AFL Grand Final winners, the Richmond Football Club, attributed its success to working with the principles of Brené Brown's core work around relationships, vulnerability and emotional safety. The club created a team ecosystem where players felt safe to be themselves.

*'A team is not a group of people who
work together. A team is a group
of people who trust each other.'*
—Simon Sinek

Survival of the most adaptable and caring

Darwin's theory of origin proposed that compassion is more instinctive than competition. His 1871 book, *The Descent of Man,* asserts that communities with the most sympathetic members will be those that thrive and flourish. [114]

Contrary to common belief, survival is not of the fittest. It is of the most adaptable, most caring and most connected. Recent research by Tomasello and others reinforce Darwin's theory and validate the interdependence and social mindedness of groups of people, highlighting the vital role of our interconnectedness. [115]

What can get easily overlooked is that we think the purpose of being kind and caring is for others' benefit. However, the research shows that being kind to others is not only good for them, it is good for us. [116] Being kind and compassionate shifts our nervous system from threat (reptile) to rest (executive) mode, where it reaps the physical and mental health benefits.

*'Our bodies are chronically in
threat mode—but being kind
recalibrates our nervous system.'*
—Dr James Doty

A toxic ego-system

When the psychological environment becomes cluttered with toxins from negative interactions and behaviours, a toxic ego-system develops. Employees become driven more by self-protection (ego) than by collaboration. The lack of trust that develops results in individuals feeling unsafe and disconnected.

We recognise that workplace ecosystems can deteriorate to poisonous levels if below-the-line behaviours are allowed to flourish unchecked. Ecosystems have the ability to tolerate the negative drag of some risk factors (or below-the-line behaviours) but when the toxins overgrow, the system becomes out of balance and the positives are not adequate to keep things thriving. If the risk factors grow unchecked, the ecosystem will be at risk of dying.

The power of leaders

Leaders are in powerful positions to cultivate the protective factors of the team environment.

As stewards of the ecosystem, leaders at every level of an organisation can take responsibility for setting the tone and standards of the psychological environment. The toxic consequences of poor workplace environments are undeniable and, as we have explored, can have tragic consequences.

Research from Safework Australia highlights that when senior leaders set a positive tone for the workplace, the ripple effect is significant.[117,118] We can see that a positive tone set by leaders is a strong protective factor. It can be a positive game-changer when it comes to the level of bullying and other poor behaviour.

One of the first steps to building a positive ecosystem is to recognise the ingredients that are vital for thriving. For many leaders, these ingredients may be hard to identify and even harder to influence. If we make the thriving ecosystem factors visible, it enables us to impact them and to engage our teams in shaping them.

In Team Acacia, there was a breakdown in trust and cooperation in the leadership team. The four key leaders stopped working collaboratively due to interpersonal tension between two of the members. The reduction in goodwill led to a lack of clear direction and leadership. The tensions on the leadership team were felt by everyone across the team, and the lack of trust became pervasive and promoted a competitive, critical and harsh environment.

Protective factors and risk factors

Protective factors and risk factors are concepts used in healthcare to describe factors that influence the chances of positive or negative outcomes. Protective factors are conditions or attributes that support growth, wellbeing and resilience by helping us deal more effectively with challenges and stress; they help us mitigate or counterbalance risk factors. Risk factors increase the likelihood of undesirable outcomes.

In order to optimise functioning and decrease the chance of negative outcomes, we try to enhance protective factors and reduce risk factors. It is like when we hear health messages about exercising more and eating less junk food, we're being encouraged to increase protective factors (exercise) and decrease risk factors (unhealthy food).

Protective factors

Research gives us clear guidelines about factors that would be protective of a thriving ecosystem. They fall into four key areas:[119]

- Leadership
- Organisational
- Workplace culture
- Employee focus.

Leadership factors

Research shows that when senior leaders set a high level of interpersonal functioning, where values like respect, trust, kindness and compassion dominate, the tone is set for the whole organisation.

A key element of capable leaders is their 'internalised' locus of control. They are not petty. Michelle Obama articulated this well, 'When they go low, we go high'. This speaks to the way above-the-line leaders do not give away power to the below-the-line behaviours of others. They do not allow another person's behaviour to determine their own. In a team, this becomes even more critical as the leader's behaviour sets the standard for all interpersonal relationships. This means that, at times, they have to rise up and step outside of any reactive responses to lead from a higher place.

What is required are key leadership skills of EI, self-awareness, self-management and self-leadership. Within the team environment, leaders use these to build a strong, positive leadership presence; they role model a strong set of behavioural standards and set a strong high road.

One of the most exemplary senior leaders I have worked with is Anika. She holds a very senior role in a large corporation and is exceptionally talented in the way she strongly models and creates a positive and hopeful environment. Anika brings a powerful level of empathy and kindness that sets a compelling tone for her colleagues. This presence is non-negotiable. Regardless of how poorly others behave, Anika always maintains her equanimity and respectfulness.

An example of this was when Anika inherited a direct report who was extremely smart and used his intellect to play subtle psychological games within their leadership team. Anika found ways to set clear boundaries. She stayed grounded and respectful in her behaviour towards him and, over time, she was able to expose his below-the-line behaviour in ways that resulted in him leaving the workplace. She had the courage to have tricky conversations and point out how his subtle behaviour was undermining the strong interpersonal fabric of the team.

A thriving workplace ecosystem needs leaders like Anika who take the interpersonal environment seriously, who are prepared to set the tone and model above-the-line behaviours, and who have the skills and courage to address interpersonal behaviours when they dip below the line.

Organisational factors

Organisational factors may be hard to differentiate from leadership skills. What I am delineating is the strategic plan: the approach of the board and C-suite leaders in setting an empowering and engaging vision and direction for the workplace. Keeping an authentic and empowered vision adds to the above-the-line ecosystem. It ensures employees have a sense of meaning and purpose, and feel valued in that they are contributing to the whole and that they are in a workplace where they can align their values.

Derek, a senior leader I worked with in a coaching capacity, had lost his focus in setting and engaging his team with its vision. He was an excellent leader in many ways; however, he expressed concern about the lack of engagement in his team. When reflecting on his challenges, he recognised that he may have prioritised good interpersonal relationships but neglected the power of regularly reconnecting with the strategic vision of the organisation and the role of his team in its fulfilment. After this coaching session, he spent part of his next team meeting reviewing and reinforcing the key elements of the team's vision. He encouraged his team to share the key elements of the vision that were most meaningful and the parts that most utilised their skills and strengths.

Derek was blown away by the powerful impact this had on the energy and output of the team. A conversation that took less than 30 minutes amplified the levels of enthusiasm and engagement in ways that lasted for some months.

Organisations that best create thriving ecosystems support leaders to lead KPIs and people. They are the types of workplaces that ensure KPIs are not at the cost of employees and they allow leaders adequate time to be people focused. Leaders need time to lead people, to form positive collegial relationships, to build psychological safety and to ensure the expectations of people are humane and reasonable. They also must find ways to influence expectations to allow employees to have a working life that is compatible with a personal life.

Workplace culture / interpersonal interaction factors

The interpersonal landscape of a thriving ecosystem is high on goodwill and psychological safety and is a learning culture. Its values are clear: respect, kindness, trust and compassion are more common than criticism, negativity and undermining.

As we've discussed in great detail, the social environment provides a neurobiological context in which we perform. When a workplace is psychologically safe, we relax. In fact, our whole nervous system relaxes and allows our higher cognitive and psychological functions to come to the fore.

I meet a lot of teams who function barely above the line or on the line but who genuinely want to soar above the line. They actively work to identify their shared values and agreed-to behaviours and then cultivate these.

In earlier chapters, we explored the psychological contract that informs the acceptable and unacceptable behaviours of the workplace. A healthy, positive psychological contract ensures that acceptable behaviours support team functioning and undesirable behaviours are seen as unacceptable.

Employee-focused factors

A workplace that places immense value on its most important asset (its employees) will be a thriving ecosystem. It will be strength-based, brain friendly and will apply evidence-based care for the staff.[120,121] Awareness of mental health, unconscious bias and diversity all provide an environment where employees feel psychologically safe and valued.

Recently, in Vietnam, I spotted a sign over the staff area that read *Happy Staff, Happy Customers* and it certainly was the vibe of the place. The staff members were friendly and helpful; they were absolutely brimming with positivity and warmth. We certainly felt the staff members were genuinely loved and cared for by the business owners.

Considering employees beyond their roles is a highly protective factor. Appreciating employees and their wellbeing ensures the organisation's expectations are not a barrier for them in having a fulfilling personal life. Asking an employee about their weekend and truly taking the time to listen and engage with the response is a highly valuable way to build connections.

Working from home during COVID-19 has given employees greater connection with and insight into the personal lives of their colleagues. In a helpful way, it has shattered the professional persona we may have thought was necessary to bring to work to bolster our credibility. The mask many of us believed we needed takes a lot of energy to maintain. Brené Brown's work is a continual reminder of the more helpful approach to unmask and to be more real and authentic.[122,123,124]

Risk factors

By creating a negative drag on the ecosystem, risk factors undermine the interpersonal fabric that we need to rely on to function well. Research highlights that there are many negative factors that create risks to the health and wellbeing of an organisation or team.[125]

Poor interpersonal environment

As we have explored, a poor interpersonal environment will be a huge risk factor to team functioning. In particular, the research on psychological safety has catapulted our awareness of the vital role of the interpersonal environment. When employees feel unable to ask for help and are fearful of asking questions (and put immense energy into impression management), it proves the psychological environment has fallen below the line. The way we treat one another at work is central to our ability to perform our roles well.

Below-the-line teams experience a lot of negative interpersonal interactions, including these tell-tale signs:

Unnecessarily critical	Self-serving ego: me before others	Employees can't be open about challenges	Excluding or isolating people	Disrespectful
Negativity	Gossiping	Unreliable	Unhelpful	Incivility
Eye-rolling	Excessive competitiveness	Defensiveness	Shaming	Controlling
Bitchiness	Inflexibility	Blaming	Impatience	Mean-spiritedness

Poor leadership practices

One of the most negative risk factors is when leaders use fear, criticism, shaming and blaming as methods for motivation or creating behavioural change. When we prioritise productivity and performance at the expense of employee wellbeing and fulfilment, we are not using positive influence. We have noted that research shows this is not a sustainable way to run any organisation.

EI has been recognised as the number one variable for successful leadership from business outcomes to positive people leadership. When organisations lack emotionally intelligent leaders, the team suffers. Leaders who lack EI often ignore or encourage below-the-line behaviours; they tend to avoid addressing poor behaviours like bullying, discrimination, harassment, shaming, blaming, defensiveness, etc. Some poor leaders even encourage these behaviours by laughing them off or trivialising employees' concerns.

Micromanagement and sacrificing employee agency for the leader's control also creates significant risk to the functioning of any team. Above-the-line leadership requires two-way accountability where employees can respectfully question their leaders, provide respectful feedback and expect mutual accountability. The absence of these adds to the risk of a deteriorating workplace ecosystem.

Poor organisational practices

Some organisations lack good human resource practices where the real rights and needs of the humans employed in the workplace go unvalued and unsupported by the department designated to this role. Lip service is paid to the policies, procedures and standards, and values are ignored despite the fancy corporate vision statements that are supposed to drive workplace standards.

Workplace structure can be unsupportive to good teamwork. An example of this is the physical environment. Immense research shows that open plan offices are poor for performance, teamwork and mental health, yet many organisations think they are a good idea without reviewing the evidence.[126] Fortunately, in a post-COVID-19 world, traditional open plan offices may become obsolete.

Despite the huge amount of accessible information, some organisations still lack awareness of how to foster a mentally healthy, inclusive workplace. When workplaces ignore the impact that mental health and wellbeing has on the work environment, it can have a severe and detrimental impact. All workplaces need a congruent set of policies, procedures and standards designed to protect the mental health and wellbeing of the workforce. There is much research that shows the benefits of this on a team environment.[127,128]

Another risk factor is when organisations have poor workforce wellbeing practices and ignore their responsibility around providing a physically and psychologically safe workplace. Many workplaces primarily offer reactive approaches such as offering employee assistance programs that are helpful but not proactive or systemic.

Revisiting Team Acacia

What were Team Acacia's protective factors?

Reflecting on Team Acacia, we can see some key protective factors even when things were below the line:

- Well-intentioned and committed professionals: It was a group of highly professional employees, extremely committed to their work.

- High-level expertise: They had exceptional skills and expertise working with some of the most complex and under-resourced individuals in the community.

- Leaders were good people: As individuals, the leaders were all respectable professionals; they were well-intentioned and well-trained in their clinical roles.

- Leaders were open to learning: The leaders were open to learning and were keen to engage in changing things for the betterment of the team and service they delivered.

What were Team Acacia's risk factors?

Team Acacia's positive and protective factors meant it was likely to be open to change and improvement. The team had so many positive factors, yet the impact of the risk factors inevitably decreased performance. Some of the risk factors were enduring and some had increased.

Over a short time, the complex interpersonal dynamics had deteriorated to the point where goodwill had evaporated. Once goodwill disappears, we tend to see other people's behaviour in a far more negative light. We can probably all relate to this. If someone whom we get along well with does something disappointing, we are more likely to cut them some slack than someone with whom we have a poor relationship.

Let's reflect on Team Acacia's risk factors:

- Leaders were not working as a team: The leaders were working at cross purposes, and although mostly well-intentioned, they were undermining each other by not conferring on decisions, not supporting each other's goals, and not trying to present a clear and mostly united front.

- Not a learning culture: As goodwill and team clarity deteriorated, it became a more tense, negative and critical environment. Employees did not feel safe with each other and stopped asking for support, stopped asking questions and stopped consulting with each other regarding challenging situations.

- One uncooperative senior staff member: One of the leaders of the team took offence to a decision the manager made, which triggered a deterioration in the working relationships of the leadership team.

- Prominent below-the-line behaviours: These included eye-rolling, shaming, excluding and bitchiness, even among the leadership and wider team.

The final risk factors are the enduring factors that will continue in this environment, even when the team is thriving.

- Heavy-duty work: The team provides services to complex and high-risk clients.

- High emotional wear and tear: The work of dealing with people who are high-risk, suicidal, substance-affected and often homeless creates significant emotional wear and tear on team members.

- Intense workload demands: The critical nature of the work, coupled with being short-staffed, creates intense and demanding workloads.

It is inevitable that every workplace will have *enduring* risk factors. No environment is perfect, but the idea is to reduce and minimise the risk factors that can be influenced.

What steps did Team Acacia take to make positive changes?

We can see that Team Acacia had been a high-performing team previously, so although the enduring factors were a challenge, we knew it wouldn't be a complete obstacle to elevate from below-the-line functioning.

The risk factors were mainly in the areas of leadership and culture. The organisational risk factors were not prominent and there had been no changes to this over recent times. The employee factors and human resource practices were quite reasonable.

The first focus of Team Acacia was to build its leadership team. This involved upskilling leaders, working with them to improve team dynamics and building their capacity to shift the culture of the broader team.

1. Building individual leadership skills

Many professionals promoted to leadership roles are technical experts, not people leaders. Team Acacia's group of leaders had some good leadership skills when things were going well, but under negative conditions they really lost their way. They had few frameworks for leadership practices and had mainly learned through trial and error. Although they had good relationships with some of their staff, they each recognised that they relied so heavily on their personal relationship skills that it was much harder to connect with direct reports with whom they did not naturally sync.

This group of leaders focused on:

- building positive relationships and camaraderie with each member of their team, regardless of how well they naturally got along
- giving team members more specific skill-based and strength-based feedback
- articulating their expectations more clearly
- modelling learning behaviours and being open about their own learning goals
- reducing the patterns of problem-solving for their employees by asking more reflective questions to draw out their employees' wisdom and knowledge.

2. Enhancing self-leadership skills

The negativity of the team reflected badly on the leaders. They all seemed self-critical and somewhat defeated. The team dynamics had undermined their confidence in themselves as leaders. Of course, as their own self-criticism was magnified, it amplified the critical way they perceived others. Situations like this easily develop into a vicious cycle, keeping positive solutions out of reach despite best intentions.

The types of skills this group of leaders focused on building included:

- better self-care and self-awareness including setting boundaries, taking lunch breaks and leaving work closer to their finish time
- valuing themselves, their skills and strengths, and finding greater appreciation for what they had to offer to their team and their service.

3. Building leadership teamwork

The biggest challenge to this team was the lack of leadership teamwork. The interpersonal dynamics had declined quite dramatically. Trust had been eroded and it was difficult for the group to find its way back to a more positive dynamic. The leadership team was not making decisions collectively, which left the rest of the team confused and disjointed.

The types of skills this group of leaders focused on building included:

- Each team member had to put their differences aside, step out of their egos and into their responsibility as the leadership team. They were willing to do this collectively.
- They each took more responsibility for being open and transparent about their differences, rather than leaving meetings bitching about other leaders.
- They also took more responsibility for supporting rather than undermining each other.

4. Building skills to communicate a consistently inspiring vision

When the leadership team was not working well, it became impossible for it to present an inspiring and cohesive vision to team members.

The types of skills this group of leaders focused on building included:

- Articulating a clear vision and making time to review that vision for the short and long term.
- Making conscious links between the day-to-day activities of the team and the larger vision, and recognising

the ways each individual's behaviours and choices progressed that vision.

5. Identifying behaviours that they value

Although the leadership team was clear on the undesirable behaviours among team members, it hadn't been explicit about the behaviours it needed its team members to engage in to bring the team above the line.

The types of skills this group of leaders focused on building included:

- Acknowledging and valuing the preferred team behaviours like cooperation, appreciation, kindness, support, having each other's back, valuing each other and assuming best intentions.
- Honing their feedback skills and having the courage to give feedback privately when they saw undesirable behaviours.

6. Making time for teamwork a priority

Teamwork doesn't just happen. It requires time; it is an investment with huge returns. One of the challenges many people have with personal and professional relationships is understanding and valuing the time and energy they need to invest. Building goodwill is like building an emotional bank account: if you invest wisely and continually put in deposits, it is easier to ride the ups and downs. It helps sustain things above the line during more turbulent and difficult times. If there is no goodwill in the bank account, things will dip below the line very quickly during difficult times.

The types of skills this group of leaders focused on building included:

- Allocating time to build team relationships through team building, social events, lunches and fun activities.
- Making regular times in meetings to talk about what the team is doing well, the vision, and how team members are progressing the team vision.

IN SUMMARY

In this chapter, we have examined the dynamics of ecosystems and how teams can be enhanced by nutrients or overwhelmed with toxins. We explored the protective factors and risk factors that can support or undermine the workplace ecosystem's capacity to thrive, and how leaders can optimise the factors at all the levels of the workplace.

In Chapter Eight, we will explore how leaders can build a thriving ecosystem and help their teams thrive.

Questions for reflection:

What are your team's nutrients?

What are your team's toxins?

In your team, what are the protective factors in each of these areas?

Leadership?

Organisational?

Workplace culture?

Employee focus?

In your team, what are the risk factors in each of these areas?

Leadership?

Organisational?

Workplace culture?

Employee focus?

Chapter Eight

BUILDING A THRIVING (ABOVE-THE-LINE) TEAM

*'They need leaders who help
them shine, who help them fulfil
their potential at work.'*
—David Rock

Ubuntu is part of a Zulu phrase that refers to the concept of community, oneness and compassion. It loosely translates to: *I am because you are.*

In some regions of South Africa, when a person does something wrong they are placed in the centre of the village where they are surrounded by their community. For two days, community members speak of all the good the 'perpetrator' has done. It is believed that each individual is fundamentally good but can sometimes make an error of judgement, which is either a cry for help or a sign of disconnection.

The community unites in this ritual to support and encourage the perpetrator to reconnect to their essential nature. The foundational belief is that connection and affirmation are much more powerful in affecting change than shame and punishment. **This is Ubuntu.** It is based on aligning with profound beliefs, values and humanity towards others; it is appreciating the interconnectedness of community, the importance of feeling valued and affirmed, and understanding the way our behaviours influence and impact each other profoundly. It is also about being so committed to one another that we are willing to help others to be at their best for the collective benefit it brings.

Questions for reflection:

How did you respond to this story?

What happens when you do the wrong thing? How do other people around you respond? How would you feel if when you did the 'wrong' thing, you were encouraged to remember yourself back in alignment with your best self?

What if when you did the wrong thing, it was perceived by yourself and others as an opportunity to learn and grow, rather than feel shame, embarrassment and judgement? How would that impact your ability to move forward?

What are your thoughts about this?

How would you feel about doing this for others? What comes up for you? What would be your resistance to doing this?

Most people would experience some reluctance to focus on the positives when someone had let them or their team down. We may not see this as fair. We may believe that being kind and positive towards someone who has erred gives them permission to keep making mistakes.

Abraham Maslow, a twentieth-century American psychologist who popularised the importance of human needs, proposed that when people appear to be something other than good and decent, it is only because they are reacting to stress, pain or the deprivation of basic human needs such as security, love and self-esteem. Although Ubuntu aligns with Maslow's theories, these ideas are underpinned by beliefs that may go against deeply held and common assumptions about humans and human behaviour.

How we hold ourselves and others accountable to standards that are good for humans is fundamental to how we live and work together. This is especially so for leaders.

Ubuntu represents a unique way to elevate these standards and promote behavioural change that is good for the individual and cultivates the workplace ecosystem.

Organisational needs

Organisations need guiding principles to direct leaders and employees towards the key skills and values that create thriving workplace communities. We need expanded consciousness and awareness, empowered leadership and ways to manage the complexity that working together generates.

Workplaces focus mainly on **what** people do and the skills they need to achieve their KPIs. Good teamwork requires a different skill set and approach. We need healthy relationships if we are to do our jobs well.

In the workplace, we need to recognise **how** employees approach their roles and teams. It is not enough to only preference individualistic KPIs; we have to value how employees relate to each other and how they work together as they perform their duties.

A psychological contract that is above the line embodies a level of psychological awareness, responsibility and safety that allows us to be authentically and fully human. It says:

- It is OK to make mistakes **BECAUSE** we can learn from them.

- We are more than our mistake **BECAUSE** we can remember that there is more to us than an error, weakness or poor judgement.
- We are not defined by our errors **BECAUSE** *errors are a momentary lapse in judgement.*
- We can remind you that there is more to you than your mistake **BECAUSE** your community can assist you to move past it.
- We have some responsibility for caring for each other **BECAUSE** caring for each other helps.
- We need to create a culture and dynamic that helps bring out the best in each other **BECAUSE** we are better together than on our own.
- Punishing, isolating, excluding or harshly judging one another because of poor performance reinforces the behaviour instead of helping the person to move away from it.

A team roadmap

This chapter reflects a roadmap that can be used to build and maintain a thriving above-the-line team environment. There are three key overarching areas we need to address:

1. **Psychological awareness** involves noticing. It is being aware of yourself and others, and of the psychological interactions, dynamics and vibe of the team. We have already explored the psychological interactions and dynamics of self-leadership and leading individuals in previous chapters.

2. **Psychological responsibility** involves the way in which leaders take responsibility for influencing and shaping relationships and dynamics in the workplace.

3. **Psychological safety** involves fostering a workplace culture that is interpersonally safe, where it's easy to be open to learning and where employees are comfortable to take the interpersonal risks of learning.

As a physical example, consider a large water spill just happened at work:

1. Awareness: *I notice the spill and recognise it.*

2. Responsibility: *It is my responsibility to do something about the spill; hence, I may work with others to address it.*

3. Safety: *It is everyone's responsibility to do everything they can to make the environment safe.*

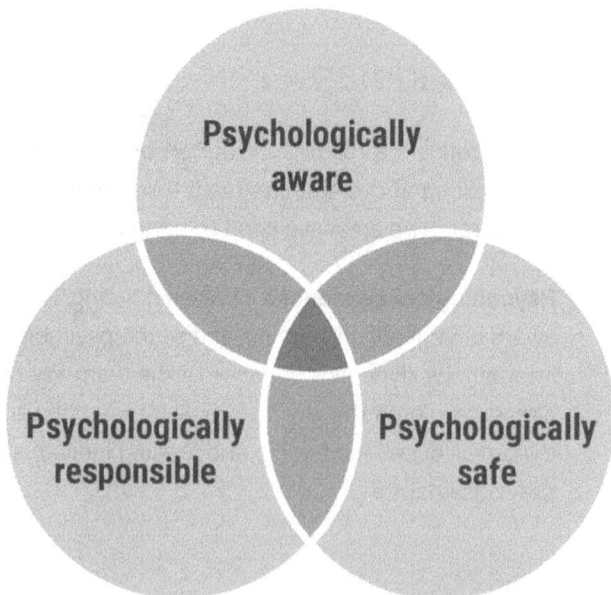

Psychological awareness

Encourage self-awareness and self-reflection

Above-the-line leaders work to increase self-awareness and self-reflection within a team environment.

Self-awareness is the foundation of an emotionally intelligent workplace. Self-reflection is the skill that builds self-awareness. It's standing back and reflecting on ourselves and on how we respond to things, how we feel about things, and how we accept and appreciate the different experiences we have that contribute to our level of self-awareness.

As we move through life, many of us build our self-awareness. Understanding ourselves at a deeper level gives us an easier platform from which to lead and guide ourselves.

The research on EI shows that self-awareness is the platform upon which all other skills of EI are built.[129,130] Within a team environment, greater self-awareness is like turning on the light so we can really see and understand what is going on. It gives much deeper and more helpful insights and perspectives.

Self-awareness requires us to look within, to go beyond the busyness of our habitual patterns of thinking and behaviours, and to reflect more deeply on our thoughts, reactions and behaviours. The unique insights this provides into ourselves and others help us navigate team dynamics more effectively.

Being willing to ask ourselves why we experience reactiveness to others' behaviour and words deepens our personal insight and, ultimately, our personal power—the power over ourselves.

Marianne Williamson says it takes courage to endure the sharp pain of self-discovery, rather than choosing to take the pain of unconsciousness that would last the rest of our lives.[131]

Increase awareness of unconscious bias

Part of building self-awareness within a psychologically healthy work environment means leaders need to become more aware of their own and their team members' interpersonal and unconscious biases. Biases work at many levels: gender, diversity, difference and cognitive.

We hold many biases that impact and influence how we function and relate to others. These biases are mostly unconscious and, as we are unaware of them, they remain hidden as to how they influence and impact our behaviour. This creates an invisible barrier to the potential of team functioning. For example, if a leader is unaware that they favour employees who are similar to them (same gender, racial background, age group, skin colour), it skews the team and reduces its optimal functioning.

If we don't recognise our bias, it can create havoc with our interactions with others and the psychological safety within the work environment. In her book, *Beat Gender Bias*, Dr Karen Morley, a psychologist and leadership coach, explores extensive research about unconscious bias.[132] She cites research that shows the more certain we are, the more likely we are to make biased decisions. She says, 'Our bias for certainty means that we tend to think that our decisions are much better than they are; we tend to dismiss the possibility that we are biased. Frustratingly, because biases operate unconsciously, it's hard to know when we are in their grip. Getting proof is tricky, and happens in retrospect, if at all. Whether you know you are biased matters less than accepting that you are likely to be biased. We could all do with being more modest, less certain, about our decisions'.

One of the most powerful ways for leaders to become aware of their bias is to be open to and invite feedback from others, rather than be defensive when feedback is given.

Another key is to reflect on some of the common forms of unconscious biases (gender, race, sexual orientation, age and disability) and consider your choices and reactions in relation to them.

Questions for reflection:

What feedback have you been given about your biases throughout your career?

Who in your team is emotionally intelligent and could give you feedback about your biases?

How safe would they feel to give you feedback about this?

Comfort zones and conscious awareness

It is easy to feel comfortable with people you agree with and harder with those you disagree with. And while we may feel more comfortable around those we agree with, our best growth occurs when we spend time with those who are different. This understanding heightens the way a psychologically safe team enables members to step outside their comfort zone and question and challenge the status quo.

We may choose to surround ourselves with employees who create an echo chamber or comfort zone where we only value the voices that reflect our own perspectives and beliefs. No doubt there needs to be some balance here: enough shared perspective so we can work together and enough difference so we can create new insights, innovation and creativity.

Awareness of core human needs, drivers and motivators

Our deepest human need is to be appreciated. Theorists, scientists and philosophers propose we have a range of core human needs. When these needs are met, we feel safe, connected, valued and fulfilled. In previous chapters, we explored how leaders can tune in to these in their one-on-one relationships with employees. At a team level, leaders need to cultivate interactions that align with our human needs.

Savvy leaders understand their teams need:

- Physical and psychological **safety**: This means they do not want any behaviours that would make others feel physically or psychologically unsafe. Hence bullying, harassment and discrimination are unlawful, but they also want to exclude the subtle below-the-line behaviours that challenge safety.

- A sense of **belonging** and social connectedness: This is vital for mental health but it also assists our nervous system to relax. Humans are wired for social belonging, and so it is unsafe when we feel isolated from the pack.

- To feel that they **matter**: Feeling valued and recognised is another strong human driver that we often seek to be met through work. Above-the-line leaders understand the importance of this and are comfortable giving their colleagues a significant amount of positive recognition.

- To feel **fulfilled**: When our need for fulfilment, meaning and purpose is considered in our working life, it supports engagement and satisfaction.

Awareness of team culture and goodwill

Goodwill in relationships is born from our core human needs being met. Think about the relationships where you feel goodwill. I'm guessing you feel safe, connected, valued and fulfilled. In our closest relationships, we can recognise that our active contribution to goodwill is what keeps our relationships thriving.

In teams, we don't need to take on a high degree of responsibility for each other but we do need to take on a high degree of responsibility for how we interact with each other. Building goodwill in a team involves interacting in ways that do not block a colleague's core human needs being met.

For example, if we bully someone, they feel unsafe. If we unnecessarily criticise someone, they feel undervalued. Our core human needs are extremely strong drivers. Experiencing the antithesis of those needs, such as when we feel unsafe, disconnected, devalued and unfulfilled, puts our mental health and wellbeing at risk.

Psychological responsibility

Express appreciation

If you're thankful, then show it.

If you're not thankful, look for opportunities to be thankful and show it.

As we've explored a lot in this book, we express the negative more often and more easily. An important and valuable component of cultivating goodwill is through being appreciative, thankful or grateful for direct reports' presence, contribution and support.

Quick to criticise, slow to praise is not a leadership style by which we want to be known.

Questions for reflection:

How do you show appreciation?

What things would you say when a direct report contributes in a positive way?

If you value someone's contribution, how would you let them know this?

If you do not commonly give positive feedback, it can feel awkward and even a little weird. Our society has often considered positive feedback in derogatory ways like someone is 'sucking up' or even worse descriptors that would not be publishable.

We are so unfamiliar with being given positive feedback that we might believe—or fear—there to be a hidden agenda. Let's say a colleague is a good anchor point for you, a good role model, someone you can learn from and someone who you feel safe with or is trustworthy. How do you tell them? When do you tell them? How do you show them?

We often think that because we feel something about someone they will automatically know, but they won't know unless you put it into words. If you value the skills, strengths and approach of a colleague, please tell them.

Collaboration over competition

Above-the-line leaders prioritise collaboration over competition.

Collaboration supports executive brain functioning; whereas, competition stimulates our lower brain functioning. As we've identified, when we're in a collaborative environment, it's good for our performance, for the quality of our thinking and for decision-making. It means we function well and it brings out the best in us.

When leaders understand how to create a team that functions above the line, they prioritise collaboration as a way to help people work together effectively, rather than playing people off against each other. Dan Siegel's work on interpersonal neurobiology reinforces this idea. His work highlights how interpersonal relationships impact brain functioning.[133] When we're in an environment that's good psychologically, we'll function at our peak—from our executive brain.

Prioritising collaboration over competition involves encouraging team members to actively work in ways that involve communication, tolerance, patience and a willingness to be authentic. The most powerful way to activate this in a team environment is to model the very behaviours you want to see.

Compassion over criticism

Compassion is an energy enhancer, whereas criticism, unchecked, feeds shame. This is one of our most corrosive and negative emotional states. Brené Brown, well-known for her famous TED talks on vulnerability and shame, suggests that shame keeps us small and safe.[134,135] It stops us taking risks and being innovative and creative. Shame is a counterproductive risk to a healthy workplace.

Feedback can be a necessary and helpful workplace process. Use feedback to look for opportunities for professional learning and building workforce capacity. However, as we've previously discussed, there is a significant difference between feedback and criticism. Feedback is focused on learning and criticism is driven by put-downs.

> Compassion in a workplace stokes the fire of peak performance ... criticism extinguishes it.

A compassionate tone is set by leaders who care for their employees, who care for their wellbeing and who care about them as people not just in terms of fulfilling their roles. Leaders facilitate this through expressing kindness and appreciating the complex humanity and diversity of their team members.

Leaders can achieve this through recognising how much they can learn from employees, and appreciating their employees as equals with wisdom, skills and knowledge. It is easy to be critical and judgemental, but it's far more helpful to team functioning to come from a place of compassion.

Connection over disconnection

Disconnection from the group triggers our human threat response. So, a key role for a leader is that of a shepherd: find ways to bring the team together. Obviously, I'm not suggesting we approach this like a border collie would: barking and snarling.

Prioritising connection means finding ways to bring people together to see how their skills can be interwoven, valued and drawn on by others within the team environment.

Nguyen, a leader of a hardworking team, adopted a focus on connection to help take his team to the next level. He began to remark on many helpful factors: how team members were similar or different; how they were complementary or had similar values, perspectives, skills and strengths; opportunities for learning and growth; and interests and vision. He brought these naturally into conversations in respectful and appropriate moments. He found the team became far more empowered and began to operate collectively beyond his expectations.

> *'One of the most important things*
> *you can do on this earth is let*
> *people know they are not alone.'*
> —Shannon L Alder

Harmony over hostility

In an orchestra, beautiful music is created by everyone playing a different role. Each instrument brings a unique quality because being the same would be counterproductive. This means that each musician needs to value the contribution and unique talent of themselves and every other musician.

> *'You don't get harmony when*
> *everybody sings the same note.'*
> —Steve Honey

Psychologically responsible leaders understand the value of each individual's contribution and the need to coach and develop people. Allowing hostility or frustration to be expressed towards others is a risk factor and damaging to the ecosystem. It is understandable that we will feel frustrated and impatient at times, but our role as leaders is to find ways to deal with this that are not directed towards others through shaming or blaming.

'Only when diverse perspectives are included, respected, and valued, can we start to get a full picture of the world.'
—Brené Brown

Assume best intentions

It's important to recognise that most people are doing the best they can. I'm not saying this about everyone, but most people. As we explored in Chapter Five, there is a very small percentage of people who are psychopathic or narcissistic and are not trustworthy in this way. It is important for you, as the leader, to be discerning and think about ways to protect yourself and your team members from those in your workplace who often operate below the line.

The challenge is choosing whether to move through life being overly cautious and not trusting everyone's good intentions. Or, do we assume that most people have good intentions; therefore, it's best for us to approach pretty much everyone with that in mind.

Assuming positive intentions from others comes easier when we trust ourselves. If we trust ourselves, it is easier to trust others. Some steps that help in assuming best intentions include:

- Giving people the benefit of the doubt.
- Trying to see things from another's perspective.
- Enquiring and asking for clarification, not automatically judging.

Commitment over compliance

> *'People don't care how much you know*
> *until they know how much you care.'*
> —Theodore Roosevelt

Do you feel that activities you are engaged in are a tick-the-box exercise? Some would say that the age of compliance may have overtaken our workplace during recent years, downgrading employee engagement and commitment. Ticking the box is a running joke in many workplaces when we're referring to activities like annual performance reviews that have lost any meaning or real purpose.

Questions for reflection:

Do you have versions of this in your workplace?

Are there ways you could breathe life back into tired routines?

How do you commit to your direct reports?

Commitment stems from authenticity, integrity and a genuine desire to contribute to others. We commit through spending time with people, giving them our attention and genuine interest, helping them take control and letting them shine and progress. The challenge to sustaining commitment often comes from ensuring we are reliable, dependable and consistent.

Health over harshness

Creating a caring workplace environment seems too simple an idea at first glance. Don't we all behave nicely? Well, no. Unfortunately, we don't.

We all have a backstory and are aware of our own inner story. But we often forget that others have backstories too.

We need to assume that not everyone is going to tell us what's going on for them. It's our job to assume that, like a large percentage of the population, they might have a lot going on currently or in the recent past. Some people have had trauma or tragedy that can take years to work through. Others have conflict in important relationships where they may be they're suffering with stress or mental health issues or they're having difficulty getting pregnant or achieving other important, but private, life goals.

'Cynicism and sarcasm are bad in person, and even worse when they travel through email and text.
—Brené Brown

This doesn't give permission for employees to be irresponsible in their roles, but it is a reminder of why we should always treat others with kindness and respect.

Let's consider two simple statistics.

1. One in five Australians of working age will deal with a mental health issue each year.
2. Almost one in two people will deal with a mental health issue in their lifetime.

These are significant statistics. These statistics will be significantly increased by the short- and long-term impacts of the COVID-19 pandemic.

Consider your work environment. How many people are in your team or are working in your vicinity? Therefore, how many people in your work environment could be dealing with a mental illness this year? Then consider the people in *their* lives. One of five of those people would also be dealing with a mental illness. Their partner, child, closest friend. That touches a large number of people. On top of this, your colleagues may be dealing with relationship breakdowns, losses, serious illnesses and the many other stressors and challenges life can throw at us.

Cultivate autonomy, adaptability and self-leadership

As we explored in Chapters Three and Four, skills in self-leadership support employees themselves as well as those with whom *they* work closely. Self-leadership does not mean *it is all about me and my universe*. Self-leaders are optimised in functioning with greater autonomy and adaptability. In a team environment, self-leaders are more likely to be givers, not takers, and to contribute cooperatively and give credit and recognition to others freely.

> *'Solve someone's problems and you produce a follower. Enable someone to solve their own problems and you produce a leader.'*
> —Alexander den Heijer

An example of how to facilitate self-leadership in team members, as Alexander den Heijer points out, is to help people help themselves. It might be quicker to solve someone else's problem but it does not facilitate generalised transferable learning.

Jane was a leader who felt very proud of her relationships with her team members; she was valued by them. However, she noticed that her direct reports continually came to her for what she perceived to be quite basic things. Being busy, Jane felt she was being helpful by quickly offering solutions that her team members seemed to value. The problem was that her direct reports fell into patterns of relying on Jane for answers. They lacked trust in themselves. Through a leadership development program, Jane realised she was doing her team members a disservice by being so helpful. She shifted gears by asking more reflective questions that invited people to find their own answers. Jane noticed it took longer in the beginning, but within a short time, she appreciated that her team was approaching her less often and had more pride in sourcing its own solutions.

Some leaders are so fearful and threatened by their employees becoming stronger than they are in any area that they discourage autonomy and foster dependence and control. I'm sure you've worked with someone like that at some point.

Courage to have tough conversations about team interactions

Having tough conversations is one of the most challenging parts of a leader's role and often one of the trickiest parts of any relationship.

Employing the right people (employees who operate above the line and are open to learning) takes us halfway there. Healthy organisations need employees who have what it takes to be team players with enough self-awareness and self-management to keep their egos in check and not spend their working hours playing out rivalry and competitiveness. Employing the right people reduces the need for too many tricky conversations.

However, there will be times when leaders need to have tough conversations about performance, attitude, approach, skill development and interpersonal interactions. Building a positive relationship helps to form a solid foundation to enable those conversations.

In Chapter Six, we explored the example of Mario who found ways to build appreciation of his team members' strengths to facilitate feedback. Taking this one step further would be having conversations about team interactions. It is our responsibility as leaders to be clear about our expectations of interpersonal interactions and dynamics. Leaders often avoid this 'hot potato' conversation as it may feel personal or uncomfortable, and yet if we do not make our expectations clear about the interpersonal environment, we risk things deteriorating below the line in times of additional pressure and stress.

Questions for reflection:

What tough conversations do you need to find the courage to have?

What tricky conversations do you tend to avoid?

Are there times you would like to provide more direct feedback about interpersonal interactions?

Tips:

1. List the feedback you would like to give to your direct reports in terms of their interpersonal interactions.

2. For each of the areas you identify, what is a skill you think your employee needs to develop?

3. How can you best support your employee to develop this skill?

4. What steps could your employee take to build this skill in bite-size chunks?

204 | LEADING ABOVE THE LINE

Psychological safety

Build protective factors and reduce risk factors

To cultivate an above-the-line culture, identify the behaviours and attitudes you want to see often, for example, collaborative, trustworthy, inclusive and encouraging.

What does an above-the-line culture look like in your work? Break it down into the following components:

- Willingness to ask for help.
- Ask questions when you need answers and to ask for help when you need assistance.
- Notice and offer to help when others are overloaded.
- Offer to teach others.
- Support others when they are overwhelmed.
- Be good at listening.
- Publicly acknowledging others.
- Listening to understand.

> *'Daring leaders work to make sure people can be themselves and feel a sense of belonging.'*
> —Brené Brown

Cultivate psychological safety and safeguard the psychological environment

As mentioned in the early chapters of the book, workplace health and safety has advanced over many decades to protect employees' physical health. We have lagged behind in ensuring work environments are psychologically safe too.

As leaders, how do we provide guidance around this? It becomes even more essential when we're talking about the team environment. It is through the team environment that we manage our individual relationships with our staff.

And what are the dynamics? What are the drivers? What are the boundaries around what is acceptable and what is unacceptable?

The psychological contract

Every relationship has a psychological contract. You have a psychological contract, healthy or unhealthy, in every relationship that you're in—including your relationship with yourself.

It is the implicit, agreed-upon way we have of operating with one another. Mostly, we do not make a psychological contract explicit and are unaware of it to a large degree but, regardless, it still exists.

Building psychological safety depends on having a healthy psychological contract and modelling below-the-line behaviours like negativity, bitchiness, bullying and gossiping are unacceptable.

At the start of this book, I referred to the distinction between organisations and how some workplace cultures are very healthy. This is because the psychological contract, the agreed-upon ways that people will behave, is completely in line with what is positive and healthy in the thriving ecosystem—this brings out the best in people.

But there are definitely some workplaces where the psychological contract is very poor; where behaviours have become unacceptable; where interactions are much more below the line;

where we're seeing more of what we might consider to be a toxic ego-system; where people are unkind to each other; and where people are disrespectful or exclude one another or bitch about each other or criticise each other unnecessarily or devalue each other.

An example of a poor psychological contract is ghosting. This can show up in a work situation where a potential candidate takes the time and energy to prepare and attend an interview but never hears back from the organisation. Ghosting can be indicative of how the psychological contract looks in that workplace.

Build a learning culture—model learning, encourage self-directed learning

> *'Every time we withhold, we rob ourselves and our colleagues of small moments of learning.'*
> —Amy Edmondson

The extensive research on psychological safety from Amy Edmondson and others challenges us to foster an environment where it is safe to learn, to ask questions, to present different ideas and opinions, and to be open to new ways of doing things.[136,137,138] The role of leaders in this environment is undeniable and pivotal. Leaders must:

1. Provide a learning framework around the work of your team. Set the scene that you are all in a continual state of learning and development, so that when mistakes are made, it is framed as part of the natural order of the work environment. It means that mistakes or errors are seen as learning opportunities, essential for growth and skill development.

2. Model being a learner. Be open about your own learning goals, share your questions and uncertainties with your team, and show the areas where you are a beginner. This provides team members with excellent modelling of how to put aside concerns of the ego and recognise that everyone is a learner regardless of their career stage or status.

3. Be vulnerable. Be OK with making mistakes and owning up. Share when you are not certain about things and where you need to get advice or more information from experts. When others are vulnerable, ask questions or own mistakes, recognise and value their willingness to learn.

4. Be curious. Asking reflective questions conveys there is learning and growth from every experience. John Dewey says we do not learn from experience ... we learn from reflecting on experience.[139] Reflective learning is a core and necessary component of adult learning. We learn from experience, regardless of whether it was a positive or negative experience. Reflecting on experience through respectful, reflective questions builds learning and understanding, and is essential for skill development and behaviour change.

Building a learning culture requires the competitive, posturing role of the ego to be set aside. This is for everyone's benefit and for the successful performance of the team. This can be one of the most central challenges for many leaders, especially those who were raised to believe that amplifying competition in teams is crucial for peak performance.

Leaders need to facilitate their team to grow collectively. They need to help team members to learn from each other, to play to their strengths, and to accept their weaknesses and vulnerabilities. Regularly enquiring about learning helps set the tone for a learning culture.

Here are some great questions to ask in team meetings:

- What did you learn this week?
- What surprised you?
- What did you learn about yourself this week?
- What did you appreciate about your team this week?

Addressing the ego in team dynamics

One, two, three, four, leave your ego at the door. It would be ideal if people who are driven by their egos walked around with a psychological mask to ensure their toxic vibes were kept to themselves.

> *'Remember teamwork begins by building trust. And the only way to do this is to overcome our need for invulnerability.'*
> —Patrick Lencioni

If you look at interactions that are negative, the common driver is ego. There are different ego dynamics at play but the general gist is of person A interacting with person B in ways to assist person A to feel better about themselves.

The drive to put someone down, in order to position ourselves more strongly within the group, alleviates some of the ego's anxiety. The act of putting others down is a defence when we don't feel good enough.

There are many possible drivers of ego, but most commonly, it is to gain personal or professional power at the expense of others. And that is what we know to be below the line.

When we can create a culture where all, or almost all, of our behaviours are good for us and for others, we'll have a thriving ecosystem rather than a toxic ego-system. The main goal is to bring everyone's behaviour together in a way that brings out the best in people.

> *'We desperately need more leaders*
> *who are committed to courageous,*
> *wholehearted leadership and who are*
> *self-aware enough to lead from their*
> *hearts, rather than unevolved leaders*
> *who lead from hurt and fear.'*
> —Brené Brown

Conclusion

SOAR
above the line

> *"As you think about your own path to daring leadership, remember Joseph Campbell's wisdom: 'The cave you fear to enter holds the treasure you seek.' Own the fear, find the cave, and write a new ending for yourself, for the people you're meant to serve and support, and for your culture. Choose courage over comfort. Choose whole hearts over armour. And choose the great adventure of being brave and afraid. At the exact same time."*
>
> —Brené Brown

Helping yourself and your team to **soar above the line** would be the best outcome of implementing the ideas contained in this book.

From an early age, I have observed a great deal of squandered potential in workplaces, schools and in our community. When we lead ourselves and others far below the line, this is the unfortunate outcome.

I'm hoping this book has inspired you to take some steps, small or big, to minimise the likelihood of this through taking greater responsibility for the psychological and interpersonal workplace environment in which you operate.

I'm grateful for the human curiosity and advances in technology, such as neuroscience, that have progressed our understanding of human needs, motivators and behaviours. In recent decades, we've made strides in making the unconscious conscious. We've forged new pathways that can advance our society and workplaces to become kinder, more civil and more psychologically responsible.

I encourage you to consider these four key steps in reshaping your workplace:

1. ***Be aware of the psychological environment:*** Understand how interpersonal relationships and behaviours influence and shape the workplace environment.
2. ***Lead yourself:*** Cultivate self-leadership to optimise your own performance, productivity and wellbeing, as well as become a powerful and positive influence for those around you.
3. ***Lead others:*** Optimise leadership of your employees with evidence-based strategies to build relationships that engage, inspire, build on strengths and create openness to learning and development.
4. ***Lead your team***: Build a thriving ecosystem, not a toxic ego-system, through optimising protective factors and reducing risk factors in ways that create a psychologically safe and thriving team.

Post-pandemic, we have a once-in-a-lifetime opportunity to reshape our workplaces. Let's lead ourselves, our employees and our workplaces to soar above the line for everyone's benefit.

Want more?

Thank you for reading *Leading Above the Line*.

My intention for writing this book was to give you a deeper understanding of workplace psychological dynamics and help you to build strategies to elevate yourself, your employees and your workplace higher above the line.

I hope this book will become a resource that you will draw upon regularly, and that you will share your learnings with others.

As this field is continually evolving, I will develop more resources and programs that will help you thrive, amplify potential and build psychological responsibility and safety in your workplaces.

Connect with Michelle

If you would like to keep in touch, you can:

1. Email me directly with your learnings and experience. I'd be delighted to hear from you and I'm always keen to hear how you are implementing and sharing your learning. michelle@michellebihary.com
2. Connect with me on LinkedIn https://www.linkedin.com/in/michellebihary/
3. Read my blog at michellebihary.com [or michellebiharyhealth.com if you're a health or community sector professional]
4. Sign up to my emailing list through my websites: michellebihary.com or michellebiharyhealth.com

Work with Michelle

I'm known for delivering game-changing programs for workplaces all over Australia and New Zealand, and for my engaging keynotes and workshops at Australian and international conferences.

I create customised programs for in-house delivery and I also have a range of public programs. These programs continue to evolve; however, as at November 2020 they include:

1. ELEVATE – Lead an Above the Line, Psychologically Safe and Thriving Team
2. People Leadership Development
3. Self-Leadership Development
4. From Risky to Robust – Leading a Psychologically Safe and Thriving Health Service
5. Professional and Workplace Resilience
6. Thriving at Work – Mental Wellbeing Matters
7. Thriving Professional Women's Program
8. Emotional Intelligence for Leaders and Customer / Client Service Roles
9. Mentoring and Professional Supervision Programs

If you think you or your team would benefit from one of my programs and you'd like to have a chat, please reach out. I am also happy to make time to discuss your needs and see if there is a match with what I can offer.

Thanks again

Michelle

michelle@michellebihary.com
www.michellebihary.com
www.michellebiharyhealth.com [for health professionals]
https://www.linkedin.com/in/michellebihary/

Glossary

Above-the-line behaviours are acceptable, healthy and responsible from a human, psychological and interpersonal perspective. They are good for people; they bring out employees' capacity to function at their best.

Below-the-line behaviours are not acceptable, healthy or responsible from a psychological and human perspective. They are not in the best interests of people and they diminish performance and wellbeing.

Brain

> **Executive brain** is the source of our best thinking and psychological functioning. It enables us to be creative, proactive and strategic, to see things from multiple perspectives, make our best decisions and be mentally and psychologically agile. The executive brain sits behind our forehead.
>
> **Brainstem / Reptile brain** becomes more active when stimulated by the amygdala when we feel unsafe or stressed. The amygdala sits above the brainstem in our limbic system. We're likely to function in more reactive and less considered ways. When our reptile brain is active, it is much harder for us to access the higher order thinking capacities of our 'executive brain'. The brainstem sits at the back of our head, down near our neck.

Interpersonal neurobiology (or **relational neurobiology**) is the emerging area of research exploring the ways interpersonal relationships and the psychological environment shape our brain and its functioning. When we're in positive relationships with our manager and team, we're far more likely to function optimally.

Neuroscience (or **neurobiology**) is the study of the nervous system, including physiology, anatomy, biology, mathematical modelling and psychology to understand neurons and neural circuits, and how these influence our functioning, learning, behaviour and relationships. Technological advances in recent years have accelerated neuroscientific research enabling us to observe the influence of neurons and neural pathways of our thinking, relationships and environment.

Neuroplasticity is the brain's ability to continually adapt and change; it is influenced by our thoughts, interactions, experiences and environment. Advances in technology highlight neuroplasticity as a dynamic process in which our brains are engaged throughout our lives. Neuroplasticity can be intentionally optimised by using our thoughts, behaviours and relationships to fulfil potential in our performance and wellbeing.

Presenteeism is when employees are at work but are not fully functioning so productivity and performance is significantly diminished. Presenteeism appears to be a much costlier problem to a workplace than absenteeism, although it is harder to observe and assess.

Psychosocial climate refers to workplace culture influenced by interpersonal and psychological factors.

Psychological contract is the implicit and unspoken agreement about what behaviours are acceptable and what behaviours are unacceptable in each relationship, team and workplace.

Psychological literacy is the ability to be aware of, understand, be reflective of and articulate one's own and others' behavioural and mental processes. People who have high psychological literacy are emotionally intelligent; they have emotional awareness of self and others, and they have emotional expression.

Psychological safety: Psychological safety as described by Amy Edmondson, Harvard Business School professor is a belief that one will not be punished or humiliated for speaking up with ideas, questions, concerns or mistakes. It refers to the psychological environment where it is safe to take the interpersonal risks of learning. Research has shown that psychological safety is the number one factor that contributes to high performance in teams.

Thriving workplace ecosystem refers to a workplace environment that is positive and healthy for humans. It naturally brings out the best in employees, and supports business success, employee performance, wellbeing and engagement.

Toxic ego-system refers to when the workplace environment is toxic and unhealthy for humans. It is driven by ego and poor interpersonal dynamics that work against employees fulfilling their potential. It can include bullying, harassment and discrimination and is below-the-line.

Further readings

Psychological safety

1. By Amy Edmonson
   The Fearless Organisation

2. Project Aristotle by Google
   https://rework.withgoogle.com/print/
   guides/5721312655835136/

3. By Dr Timothy R Clark
   The 4 stages of Psychological Safety

Positive neuroplasticity and interpersonal neurobiology

1. *By Dr Daniel Siegel*
   Interpersonal Neurobiology
   Mindsight

2. By Rick Hanson
   Resilient
   Neurodharma
   Buddha's Brain

Emotional intelligence

1. All books by Daniel Goleman
2. *Emotional Intelligence 2.0* by Travis Bradberry
3. Genos International by www.genosinternational.com

Psychological references

1. By Brene Brown
   I Thought it was just Me
   The Gifts of Imperfection
   Dare to Lead

2. By Kristin Neff
   Self-compassion

3. By Martin Seligman
   Flourish
   Character Strengths and Virtues
   Learned Optimism
   Authentic Happiness

4. By Ken Wilber
   Integral Psychology
   A Brief History of Everything

5. By Dr David Hawkins
   Power vs Force

6. By Michael Henderson
   Above the Line

7. By Andrew Bryant and Ana Lucia Kazan
   Self-Leadership

8. By Mihaly Csikszentmihaly
   Flow

Teams and organisations

1. By Patrick Lencioni
   The Five Dysfunctions of a Team

2. By Bolman and Deal
   Reframing Organisations

3. By Peter Senge
   The Fifth Discipline
   Presence

Endnotes

1. Deloitte. (2017, March). *At a tipping point? Workplace mental health and wellbeing.* ttps://www2.deloitte.com/uk/en/pages/public-sector/articles/workplace-mental-health-and-wellbeing.html

2. McKenty, J. (2018, November 12). *Struggling With High Performance Teams? You Might Need Some Brain Science.* Forbes. https://www.forbes.com/sites/joshmckenty/2018/11/12/struggling-with-high-performance-teams-you-might-need-some-brain-science/#58d3670b3601

3. Hunt, V. (2020, February 14). *Why diversity matters.* McKinsey & Company. https://www.mckinsey.com/business-functions/organization/our-insights/why-diversity-matters

4. Remley, D. (2017). *Managerial Communication and the Brain.* Business Expert Press.

5. Borysenko, K. (2019, June 3). *Burnout Is Now An Officially Diagnosable Condition: Here's What You Need To Know About It.* Forbes. https://www.forbes.com/sites/karlynborysenko/2019/05/29/burnout-is-now-an-officially-diagnosable-condition-heres-what-you-need-to-know-about-it/#416513212b99

6. Deloitte. (2017, March). *At a tipping point? Workplace mental health and wellbeing.* https://www2.deloitte.com/uk/en/pages/public-sector/articles/workplace-mental-health-and-wellbeing.html

7. Chapman, S., Kangasniemi, A., Maxwell, L., & Sereneo, M. (n.d.). *The ROI in workplace mental health programs: Good for people, good for business.* Deloitte. https://www2.deloitte.com/content/dam/Deloitte/ca/Documents/about-deloitte/ca-en-about-blueprint-for-workplace-mental-health-final-aoda.pdf

8. Hunt, V. (2020b, February 14). *Why diversity matters.* McKinsey & Company. https://www.mckinsey.com/business-functions/organization/our-insights/why-diversity-matters

9. Youssef, C. M., & Luthans, F. (2007). Positive Organizational Behavior in the Workplace. *Journal of Management, 33*(5), 774–800. https://doi.org/10.1177/0149206307305562

10. Farr-Wharton, B., Shacklock, K., Brunetto, Y., Teo, S. T. T., & Farr-Wharton, R. (2017). Workplace bullying, workplace relationships and job outcomes for police officers in Australia. *Public Money & Management, 37*(5), 325–332. https://doi.org/10.1080/09540962.2017.1328180

11. Anjum, A., Ming, X., Siddiqi, A., & Rasool, S. (2018). An Empirical Study Analyzing Job Productivity in Toxic Workplace Environments. *International Journal of Environmental Research and Public Health, 15*(5), 1035. https://doi.org/10.3390/ijerph15051035

12. Duffy, M. and Yamada, D., 2018. *Workplace Bullying And Mobbing In The United States*. Praeger.

13. Wilkerson, J. (2019). Chronic Underfit of the Small Firm's HRM Function: When Low Functional Elaboration Interacts with Contingencies. *Journal of Organizational Psychology, 19*(2), 161–167. https://doi.org/10.33423/jop.v19i2.2051

14. Koehn, P. H. (2010). Linking China, India, and the United States. *International Studies Review, 12*(2), 331–334. https://doi.org/10.1111/j.1468-2486.2010.00940.x

15. Ngo, C. (2019, June 5). *Top challenges for HR in start-ups*. HR Advance. https://hradvance.com.au/news-articles/start-up-challenges-for-hr

16. Deloitte. (2017, March). *At a tipping point? Workplace mental health and wellbeing*. https://www2.deloitte.com/uk/en/pages/public-sector/articles/workplace-mental-health-and-wellbeing.html

17. Dollard, M., Bailey, T., McLinton, S., Richards, P., McTernan, W., Taylor, A., & Bond, S. (2012, December). *The Australian workplace barometer: Report on psychosocial safety climate and worker health in Australia*. Safe Work Australia. https://www.safeworkaustralia.gov.au/system/files/documents/1702/the-australian-workplace-barometer-report.pdf

18. Scheepers, R. A., Boerebach, B. C. M., Arah, O. A., Heineman, M. J., & Lombarts, K. M. J. M. H. (2015). A Systematic Review of the Impact

of Physicians' Occupational Well-Being on the Quality of Patient Care. *International Journal of Behavioural Medicine, 22*(6), 683–698. https://doi.org/10.1007/s12529-015-9473-3

19. Haque, M. A., Fernando, M., & Caputi, P. (2015). *The mediating role of employee turnover intentions on the relationship between HR practices and presenteeism: Evidence from Australian employees.* University of Wollongong Australia. https://scholars.uow.edu.au/display/publication104817

20. Maroney, J. (2019, February 26). *Corrosive Effects of Unplanned Absenteeism on Retailers.* The Workforce Institute at Kronos. https://workforceinstitute.org/effects-of-unplanned-absenteeism-on-retailers/

21. Pfeffer, J. (2018). *Dying for a Paycheck: How Modern Management Harms Employee Health and Company Performance and What We Can Do About It.* Harper Business.

22. Leach, L. S., Too, L. S., Batterham, P. J., Kiely, K. M., Christensen, H., & Butterworth, P. (2020). Workplace Bullying and Suicidal Ideation: Findings from an Australian Longitudinal Cohort Study of Mid-Aged Workers. *International Journal of Environmental Research and Public Health, 17*(4), 1448. https://doi.org/10.3390/ijerph17041448

23. Milner, A. J., Spittal, M. J., & Bismark, M. M. (2017). Suicide by health professionals: a retrospective mortality study in Australia, 2001–2012. *Medical Journal of Australia, 206*(11), 506. https://doi.org/10.5694/mja16.01372

24. Victoria State Government. (n.d.). *Bullying - Brodie's Law.* State of Victoria, Australia. https://www.justice.vic.gov.au/safer-communities/crime-prevention/bullying-brodies-law

25. Thomas, A. (2017, September 20). Why working fewer hours would make us more productive. *The Guardian.* https://www.theguardian.com/sustainable-business/2015/nov/09/fewer-working-hours-doctors-eu-negotiations

26. London, A. A. C. W. I. (2016, March 31). Get a life. *The Economist.* https://www.economist.com/free-exchange/2013/09/24/get-a-life

27. Productive hours - OECD Observer. (2012). *Observer.* https://oecdobserver.org/news/fullstory.php/aid/3841/Productive_hours.html

28. Crouch, D. (2017, November 29). Efficiency up, turnover down: Sweden experiments with six-hour working day. *The Guardian.* https://www.theguardian.com/world/2015/sep/17/efficiency-up-turnover-down-sweden-experiments-with-six-hour-working-day

29. *Laker, B., & Roulet, T. (2019, August 5). Will the 4-Day Workweek Take Hold in Europe? Harvard Business Review. https://hbr. org/2019/08/will-the-4-workweek-take-hold-in-europe*

30. Glaveski, S. (2018, December 11). *The Case for the 6-Hour Workday.* Harvard Business Review. https://hbr.org/2018/12/the-case-for-the-6-hour-workday

31. Schwartz, J., Jones, R., Hatfield, S., & Anderson, S. (2019, April 1). *What is the future of work?* Deloitte Insights. https://www2.deloitte. com/global/en/insights/focus/technology-and-the-future-of-work/ redefining-work-workforces-workplaces.html

32. Chapman, S., Kangasniemi, A., Maxwell, L., & Sereneo, M. (n.d.). *The ROI in workplace mental health programs: Good for people, good for business.* Deloitte. https://www2.deloitte.com/content/dam/Deloitte/ ca/Documents/about-deloitte/ca-en-about-blueprint-for-workplace-mental-health-final-aoda.pdf

33. Peñarredonda, J. L. (2018). *Yes, you should really "be yourself" at work.* BBC Worklife. https://www.bbc.com/worklife/article/20181129-yes-you-should-really-be-yourself-at-work

34. Becher, H., Dollard, M., Asia Pacific Centre for Work and Health Safety, WHO Collaborating Centre in Occupational Health, & University of South Australia. (2016, November). *Psychosocial Safety Climate and Better Productivity in Australian Workplaces.* Safe Work Australia. https://www.safeworkaustralia.gov.au/doc/psychosocial-safety-climate-and-better-productivity-australian-workplaces-costs-productivity

35. Dollard, M., Bailey, T., McLinton, S., Richards, P., McTernan, W., Taylor, A., & Bond, S. (2012, December). *The Australian Workplace Barometer: Report on Psychosocial Safety Climate And Worker Health In Australia.* Safe Work Australia. https://www.safeworkaustralia.gov.au/system/files/documents/1702/the-australian-workplace-barometer-report.pdf

36. House, .c.C.P.A. (2017, January 16). *Chapter 3*. Parliament of Australia. https://www.aph.gov.au/Parliamentary_Business/Committees/Senate/Community_Affairs/MedicalComplaints45/Report/c03

37. Lewin, E. (2019, June 26). *More trainee doctors removed from hospitals over concerns for their welfare*. NewsGP. https://www1.racgp.org.au/newsgp/gp-opinion/more-trainee-doctors-removed-from-hospitals-over-c

38. Aubusson, K. (2019, June 19). *Third major Sydney hospital unit banned from training junior doctors*. The Sydney Morning Herald. https://www.smh.com.au/national/nsw/third-major-sydney-hospital-unit-banned-from-training-junior-doctors-20190619-p51z9m.html

39. Groth, M. (2019, February 20). *How aggression and bullying drain hospital capability*. UNSW BusinessThink. https://www.businessthink.unsw.edu.au/articles/how-aggression-and-bullying-drain-hospital-capability

40. Maslow, A. H. (2013). *A Theory of Human Motivation*. Martino Fine Books.

41. Ph.D, H. R., & Hanson, F. (2020). *Resilient: How to Grow an Unshakable Core of Calm, Strength, and Happiness* (Reprint ed.). Harmony.

42. *Work-related stress, anxiety or depression statistics in Great Britain, 2019*. (19-10). Health & Safety Executive. https://www.hse.gov.uk/statistics/causdis/stress.pdf

43. *Work-Related Mental Disorders Profile*. (2015). Safe Work Australia. https://www.safeworkaustralia.gov.au/system/files/documents/1702/work-related-mental-disorders-profile.pdf

44. Becher, H., Dollard, M., Asia Pacific Centre for Work and Health Safety, WHO Collaborating Centre in Occupational Health, & University of South Australia. (2016, November). *Psychosocial Safety Climate and Better Productivity in Australian Workplaces*. Safe Work Australia. https://www.safeworkaustralia.gov.au/doc/psychosocial-safety-climate-and-better-productivity-australian-workplaces-costs-productivity

45. Chapman, S., Kangasniemi, A., Maxwell, L., & Sereneo, M. (n.d.). *The ROI in workplace mental health programs: Good for people, good for*

business. Deloitte. https://www2.deloitte.com/content/dam/Deloitte/ca/Documents/about-deloitte/ca-en-about-blueprint-for-workplace-mental-health-final-aoda.pdf

46. Beyond Blue. (2014). *Heads Up Initiative: Employer of Choice Study*. Instinct and Reason. https://www.headsup.org.au/docs/default-source/resources/instinct_and_reason_employer_of_choice.pdf?sfvrsn=4

47. Chapman, S., Kangasniemi, A., Maxwell, L., & Sereneo, M. (n.d.). *The ROI in workplace mental health programs: Good for people, good for business*. Deloitte. https://www2.deloitte.com/content/dam/Deloitte/ca/Documents/about-deloitte/ca-en-about-blueprint-for-workplace-mental-health-final-aoda.pdf

48. Moss, J. (2019, December 16). *Burnout Is About Your Workplace, Not Your People*. Harvard Business Review. https://hbr.org/2019/12/burnout-is-about-your-workplace-not-your-people

49. Argyris, C. (1960). *Understanding Organizational Behavior*. The Dorsey Press.

50. "The term 'middle prefrontal cortex' includes the medial, orbitofrontal, and ventrolateral regions." Siegel, D. J. (2009). Mindful awareness, mindsight, and neural integration. *The Humanistic Psychologist, 37*(2), 137–158. https://doi.org/10.1080/08873260902892220

51. Stephen Dimmock is an associate professor of finance at the Nanyang Business School at Nanyang Technological University in Singapore. William C. Gerken is an assistant professor at the Gatton College of Business and Economics at the University of Kentucky. Dimmock, S., & Gerken, W. (2018, March 14). *Research: How One Bad Employee Can Corrupt a Whole Team*. Harvard Business Review. https://hbr.org/2018/03/research-how-one-bad-employee-can-corrupt-a-whole-team

52. Edmondson, A. (1999). Psychological Safety and Learning Behavior in Work Teams. *Administrative Science Quarterly, 44*(2), 350. https://doi.org/10.2307/2666999

53. M.D., D. S. J. (2012). *Pocket Guide to Interpersonal Neurobiology: An Integrative Handbook of the Mind (Norton Series on Interpersonal Neurobiology)* (Thrid Printing Used ed.). W. W. Norton & Company.

54. Edmondson, A. C. (2018). *The Fearless Organization: Creating Psychological Safety in the Workplace for Learning, Innovation, and Growth* (1st ed.). Wiley.

55. Writer, S. (n.d.). *Human Resources Online.* Https://Www. Humanresourcesonline.Net/. https://www.humanresourcesonline. net/4-drivers-of-psychological-safety-at-the-workplace

56. Edmondson, A. (1999). Psychological Safety and Learning Behavior in Work Teams. *Administrative Science Quarterly, 44*(2), 350. https:// doi.org/10.2307/2666999

57. Edmondson, A. C. (2018). *The Fearless Organization: Creating Psychological Safety in the Workplace for Learning, Innovation, and Growth* (1st ed.). Wiley.

58. Google. (n.d.). *re:Work.* https://rework.withgoogle.com/print/ guides/5721312655835136/

59. Vaish, A., Grossmann, T., & Woodward, A. (2008). Not all emotions are created equal: The negativity bias in social-emotional development. *Psychological Bulletin, 134*(3), 383–403. https://doi.org/10.1037/0033-2909.134.3.383

60. Goleman, D. (2005). *Emotional Intelligence: Why It Can Matter More Than IQ* (10th Anniversary ed.). Bantam.

61. Bryant, A., & Kazan, A. L. (2012). *Self-Leadership: How to Become a More Successful, Efficient, and Effective Leader from the Inside Out* (1st ed.). McGraw-Hill Education.

62. Blanchard, K. (2020). *Developing Self-Leaders: A Competitive Advantage for Organizations.* The Ken Blanchard Companies. https:// resources.kenblanchard.com/whitepapers/developing-self-leaders

63. The *'Self-leadership' approach* report can be downloaded on the European Commission official website. European Commission. (2017, March). *European Commission.* https://ec.europa.eu/

64. Rozin, P., & Royzman, E. B. (2001). Negativity Bias, Negativity Dominance, and Contagion. *Personality and Social Psychology Review, 5*(4), 296–320. https://doi.org/10.1207/s15327957pspr0504_2

65. ® *accreditation | Strengths development training.* (2020, September 9). Strengthscope. https://www.strengthscope.com/hr-training/

66. Sinek, S. (2011). *Start with Why: How Great Leaders Inspire Everyone to Take Action* (Reprint ed.). Portfolio.

67. TED. (2009, September 1). *How great leaders inspire action* [Video]. TED Talks. https://www.ted.com/talks/simon_sinek_how_great_leaders_inspire_action?language=en

68. Morrissey, M. (2016, June 16). *What Gandhi wants you to know about the power of positive thinking.* Huffpost. https://www.huffpost.com/entry/what-gandhi-wants-you-to-know-about-the-power-of-positive-thinking_b_10487524

69. Hanson, R. (n.d.). *The Positive Neuroplasticity Training.* Rick Hanson, Ph.D. https://courses.rickhanson.net/courses/the-positive-neuroplasticity-training

70. Hanson, R. (2018, November 8). *Positive Neuroplasticity.* Dr. Rick Hanson. https://www.rickhanson.net/articles/positive-neuroplasticity/

71. Positive neuroplasticity is 'the physiological ability of the brain to form and strengthen dendritic connections, produce beneficial morphological changes, and increase cognitive reserve.' Vance, D. E., Roberson, A. J., McGuinness, T. M., & Fazeli, P. L. (2010). How Neuroplasticity and Cognitive Reserve Protect Cognitive Functioning. *Journal of Psychosocial Nursing and Mental Health Services, 48*(4), 23–30. https://doi.org/10.3928/02793695-20100302-01

72. Hanson, R. (2018, November 8). *Positive Neuroplasticity.* Dr. Rick Hanson. https://www.rickhanson.net/articles/positive-neuroplasticity/

73. Hanson, R. (n.d.). *The Positive Neuroplasticity Training.* Rick Hanson, Ph.D. https://courses.rickhanson.net/courses/the-positive-neuroplasticity-training

74. Hanson, R. (2018, November 8). *Positive Neuroplasticity.* Dr. Rick Hanson. https://www.rickhanson.net/articles/positive-neuroplasticity/

75. Interpersonal Neurobiology, also known as relational neuroscience, is a theory and model that describes human development and functioning. It describes how the brain and mind are shaped in the context of relationships. Siegal, D. (n.d.). *Dr. Dan Siegel - About - Interpersonal Neurobiology*. Dr. Dan Siegel. https://www.drdansiegel.com/about/interpersonal_neurobiology/

76. Caprino, K. (2018, December 20). *How To Build Work Cultures Of Psychological Safety Rather Than Fear*. Forbes. https://www.forbes.com/sites/kathycaprino/2018/12/20/how-to-build-work-cultures-of-psychological-safety-rather-than-fear/#21f801996f69

77. *Study Reveals That A Bad Boss Can Make Employees Sick*. (2018, December 6). Apost. https://www.apost.com/en/blog/study-reveals-that-a-bad-boss-can-make-employees-sick/440/?un_id=1543623068251&utm_source=fb&utm_medium=fb_1503815046562182_apost_en&utm_term=USA_en&utm_campaign=blog_440&utm_content=631

78. Gallup's comprehensive 2015 study, *The State of the American Manager*, found 50% of Americans have left a job to 'get away from their manager at some point in their career'. Gallup, Inc. (2020, June 18). *State of the American Manager*. Gallup.Com. https://www.gallup.com/services/182138/state-american-manager.aspx

79. A study found workplace incivilities have the potential to not only negatively affect an employee's sleep but their partner's as well. Portland State University. (2018, December 14). *A co-worker's rudeness can affect your sleep -- and your partner's*. ScienceDaily. https://www.sciencedaily.com/releases/2018/12/181214093825.htm

80. Han, G. H., Harms, P. D., & Bai, Y. (2015). Nightmare Bosses: The Impact of Abusive Supervision on Employees' Sleep, Emotions, and Creativity. *Journal of Business Ethics, 145*(1), 21–31. https://doi.org/10.1007/s10551-015-2859-y

81. Demsky, C. A., Fritz, C., Hammer, L. B., & Black, A. E. (2019). Workplace incivility and employee sleep: The role of rumination and recovery experiences. *Journal of Occupational Health Psychology, 24*(2), 228–240. https://doi.org/10.1037/ocp0000116

82. Cherniss, C., Goleman, D., & Bennis, W. (2001). *The Emotionally Intelligent Workplace: How to Select For, Measure, and Improve Emotional Intelligence in Individuals, Groups, and Organizations* (1st ed.). Jossey-Bass.

83. Stough, C., Saklofske, D. H., & Parker, J. D. A. (2010). *Assessing Emotional Intelligence: Theory, Research, and Applications (The Springer Series on Human Exceptionality)* (Softcover reprint of hardcover 1st ed. 2009 ed.). Springer.

84. Bowlby;, J. (2020). *A Secure Base; Clinical Applications of Attachment Theory by John Bowlby (1988-05-05)*. Routledge; First Edition edition (1988-05-05).

85. Saunders, E. G. (2019, March 29). *The 4 'Attachment Styles,' and How They Sabotage Your Work-Life Balance*. https://www.nytimes.com/2018/12/19/smarter-living/attachment-styles-work-life-balance.html.

86. Richards, D. A., & Schat, A. C. H. (2011). Attachment at (not to) work: Applying attachment theory to explain individual behavior in organizations. *Journal of Applied Psychology, 96*(1), 169–182. https://doi.org/10.1037/a0020372

87. Lin, C. (2009, December 11). *Modeling Corporate Citizenship, Organizational Trust, and Work Engagement Based on Attachment Theory*. Journal of Business Ethics. https://link.springer.com/article/10.1007/s10551-010-0364-x

88. Chamorro-Premuzic, T. C. (2019, April 9). *1 in 5 business leaders may have psychopathic tendencies – here's why, according to a psychology professor*. CNBC. https://www.cnbc.com/2019/04/08/the-science-behind-why-so-many-successful-millionaires-are-psychopaths-and-why-it-doesnt-have-to-be-a-bad-thing.html

89. APS. (2016, September 13). *Corporate psychopaths common and can wreak havoc in business, researcher says*. https://www.psychology.org.au/news/media_releases/13September2016/Brooks/

90. Gillespie, D. (2017). *Taming toxic people: The science of identifying and dealing with psychopaths at home & at work*. Pam Macmillan Australia.

91. Baumeister, R. F., Bratslavsky, E., Finkenauer, C., & Vohs, K. D. (2001). Bad is Stronger than Good. *Review of General Psychology, 5*(4), 323–370. https://doi.org/10.1037/1089-2680.5.4.323

92. Hall, A. (2020, April 23). *Iceland Bans Sociopaths From Government*. Laughing in Disbelief. https://www.patheos.com/blogs/laughingindisbelief/2020/04/iceland-bans-sociopaths-from-government/

93. Siegel, D. (n.d.). *Dr. Dan Siegel - About - Interpersonal Neurobiology*. Dr. Dan Siegel. https://www.drdansiegel.com/about/interpersonal_neurobiology/ Interpersonal Neurobiology, also known as relational neuroscience, is a theory and model that describes human development and functioning. It describes how the brain and mind are shaped in the context of relationships.

94. Dollard, M., Bailey, T., McLinton, S., Richards, P., McTernan, W., Taylor, A., & Bond, S. (2012, December). *The Australian Workplace Barometer: Report on Psychosocial Safety Climate And Worker Health In Australia*. Safe Work Australia. https://www.safeworkaustralia.gov.au/system/files/documents/1702/the-australian-workplace-barometer-report.pdf

95. LaMontagne, A. D. (2008, May 27). *Job strain — Attributable depression in a sample of working Australians: Assessing the contribution to health inequalities*. BMC Public Health. https://bmcpublichealth.biomedcentral.com/articles/10.1186/1471-2458-8-181

96. Department for Work and Pensions. (2017, November 30). *Thriving at Work: a review of mental health and employers*. GOV.UK. https://www.gov.uk/government/publications/thriving-at-work-a-review-of-mental-health-and-employers

97. Edmondson, A. (1999). Psychological Safety and Learning Behavior in Work Teams. *Administrative Science Quarterly, 44*(2), 350. https://doi.org/10.2307/2666999

98. Edmondson, A. C. (2018). *The Fearless Organization: Creating Psychological Safety in the Workplace for Learning, Innovation, and Growth* (1st ed.). Wiley.

99. Google. (n.d.). *re:Work*. https://rework.withgoogle.com/print/guides/5721312655835136/

100. Aldag, R., & Reschke, W. (1997). *Employee Value Added: Measuring Discretionary Effort and Its Value to the Organization*. Center for Organization Effectiveness, Inc. http://citeseerx.ist.psu.edu/viewdoc/download?doi=10.1.1.618.6993&rep=rep1&type=pdf

101. Lloyd, R. (2008). Discretionary Effort and the Performance Domain. *The Australian and New Zealand Journal of Organisational Psychology, 1*, 22–34. https://doi.org/10.1375/ajop.1.1.22

102. RSA. (2010, April 1). *RSA ANIMATE: Drive: The surprising truth about what motivates us*. YouTube. https://www.youtube.com/watch?v=u6XAPnuFjJc

103. Gallup, Inc. (2017). *State of the Global Workplace*. Gallup.Com. https://www.gallup.com/workplace/238079/state-global-workplace-2017.aspx

104. Stough, C., Saklofske, D. H., & Parker, J. D. A. (2010). *Assessing Emotional Intelligence: Theory, Research, and Applications (The Springer Series on Human Exceptionality)* (Softcover reprint of hardcover 1st ed. 2009 ed.). Springer.

105. Stough, C., Saklofske, D. H., & Parker, J. D. A. (2010). *Assessing Emotional Intelligence: Theory, Research, and Applications (The Springer Series on Human Exceptionality)* (Softcover reprint of hardcover 1st ed. 2009 ed.). Springer.

106. Siegel, D. (n.d.). *Dr. Dan Siegel - About - Interpersonal Neurobiology*. Dr. Dan Siegel. https://www.drdansiegel.com/about/interpersonal_neurobiology/

107. Negativity bias refers to our proclivity to 'attend to, learn from, and use negative information far more than positive information'. Vaish, A., Grossmann, T., & Woodward, A. (2008b). Not all emotions are created equal: The negativity bias in social-emotional development. *Psychological Bulletin, 134*(3), 383–403. https://doi.org/10.1037/0033-2909.134.3.383

108. Negative bias is an 'asymmetry' in the way we process negative and positive. 'Negative events elicit more rapid and more prominent responses than non-negative events.' Carretié, L., Mercado, F., Tapia, M., & Hinojosa, J. A. (2001). Emotion, attention, and the 'negativity bias', studied through event-related potentials. *International Journal*

of Psychophysiology, 41(1), 75–85. https://doi.org/10.1016/s0167-8760(00)00195-1

109. Losada, M., & Heaphy, E. (2004). The Role of Positivity and Connectivity in the Performance of Business Teams. *American Behavioral Scientist, 47*(6), 740–765. https://doi.org/10.1177/0002764203260208

110. Corporate Executive Board. (2002). *Building the High-Performance Workforce: A Quantitative Analysis of the Effectiveness of Performance Management Strategies*. Corporate Leadership Council. https://marble-arch-online-courses.s3.amazonaws.com/CLC_Building_the_High_Performance_Workforce_A_Quantitative_Analysis_of_the_Effectiveness_of_Performance_Management_Strategies1.pdf

111. Losada, M., & Heaphy, E. (2004b). The Role of Positivity and Connectivity in the Performance of Business Teams. *American Behavioral Scientist, 47*(6), 740–765. https://doi.org/10.1177/0002764203260208

112. Corporate Executive Board. (2002). *Building the High-Performance Workforce: A Quantitative Analysis of the Effectiveness of Performance Management Strategies*. Corporate Leadership Council. https://marble-arch-online-courses.s3.amazonaws.com/CLC_Building_the_High_Performance_Workforce_A_Quantitative_Analysis_of_the_Effectiveness_of_Performance_Management_Strategies1.pdf

113. Siegel, D. (n.d.). *Dr. Dan Siegel - About - Interpersonal Neurobiology*. Dr. Dan Siegel. https://www.drdansiegel.com/about/interpersonal_neurobiology/

114. Darwin, C. (2019). *The Descent of Man*. Digireads.com Publishing.

115. Tomasello, M. (2001). *The Cultural Origins of Human Cognition* (Reprint ed.). Harvard University Press.

116. Chancellor, J., Margolis, S., Jacobs Bao, K., & Lyubomirsky, S. (2018). Everyday prosociality in the workplace: The reinforcing benefits of giving, getting, and glimpsing. *Emotion, 18*(4), 507–517. https://doi.org/10.1037/emo0000321

117.	*Psychosocial safety climate and better productivity in Australian workplaces: Costs, productivity, presenteeism, absenteeism | Safe Work Australia.* (2016, November 23). Safe Work Australia. https://www.safeworkaustralia.gov.au/doc/psychosocial-safety-climate-and-better-productivity-australian-workplaces-costs-productivity

118.	Chapman, S., Kangasniemi, A., Maxwell, L., & Sereneo, M. (n.d.). *The ROI in workplace mental health programs: Good for people, good for business.* Deloitte. https://www2.deloitte.com/content/dam/Deloitte/ca/Documents/about-deloitte/ca-en-about-blueprint-for-workplace-mental-health-final-aoda.pdf

119.	Plimmer, G., Proctor-Thomson, S., Donnelly, N., & Sim, D. (2017). The mistreatment of public service workers: identifying key risk and protective factors. *Public Money & Management, 37*(5), 333–340. https://doi.org/10.1080/09540962.2017.1328186

120.	*Psychosocial safety climate and better productivity in Australian workplaces: Costs, productivity, presenteeism, absenteeism | Safe Work Australia.* (2016, November 23). Safe Work Australia. https://www.safeworkaustralia.gov.au/doc/psychosocial-safety-climate-and-better-productivity-australian-workplaces-costs-productivity

121.	Chapman, S., Kangasniemi, A., Maxwell, L., & Sereneo, M. (n.d.). *The ROI in workplace mental health programs: Good for people, good for business.* Deloitte. https://www2.deloitte.com/content/dam/Deloitte/ca/Documents/about-deloitte/ca-en-about-blueprint-for-workplace-mental-health-final-aoda.pdf

122.	Brown, B. (2018). *Dare to Lead: Brave Work. Tough Conversations. Whole Hearts.* (First Edition). Random House.

123.	Peñarredonda, J. L. (2018). *Yes, you should really "be yourself" at work.* BBC Worklife. https://www.bbc.com/worklife/article/20181129-yes-you-should-really-be-yourself-at-work

124.	Hunt, V. (2020, February 14). *Why diversity matters.* McKinsey & Company. https://www.mckinsey.com/business-functions/organization/our-insights/why-diversity-matters

125.	Plimmer, G., Proctor-Thomson, S., Donnelly, N., & Sim, D. (2017). The mistreatment of public service workers: identifying key risk and

protective factors. *Public Money & Management, 37*(5), 333–340.
https://doi.org/10.1080/09540962.2017.1328186

126. Joshi, V. (2018, October 19). *Are Open-Plan Offices Really The Way Forward?* Entrepreneur. https://www.entrepreneur.com/article/321993

127. *Psychosocial safety climate and better productivity in Australian workplaces: Costs, productivity, presenteeism, absenteeism | Safe Work Australia.* (2016, November 23). Safe Work Australia. https://www.safeworkaustralia.gov.au/doc/psychosocial-safety-climate-and-better-productivity-australian-workplaces-costs-productivity

128. Chapman, S., Kangasniemi, A., Maxwell, L., & Sereneo, M. (n.d.). *The ROI in workplace mental health programs: Good for people, good for business.* Deloitte. https://www2.deloitte.com/content/dam/Deloitte/ca/Documents/about-deloitte/ca-en-about-blueprint-for-workplace-mental-health-final-aoda.pdf

129. Stough, C., Saklofske, D. H., & Parker, J. D. A. (2010). *Assessing Emotional Intelligence: Theory, Research, and Applications (The Springer Series on Human Exceptionality)* (Softcover reprint of hardcover 1st ed. 2009 ed.). Springer.

130. Cherniss, C., Goleman, D., & Bennis, W. (2001). *The Emotionally Intelligent Workplace: How to Select For, Measure, and Improve Emotional Intelligence in Individuals, Groups, and Organizations* (1st ed.). Jossey-Bass.

131. Williamson, M. (1996). *A Return to Love: Reflections on the Principles of "A Course in Miracles"* (Reissue ed.). HarperOne.

132. Morley, K. (2020). *Beat Gender Bias.* Major Street Publishing.

133. Siegel, D. (n.d.). *Dr. Dan Siegel - About - Interpersonal Neurobiology.* Dr. Dan Siegel. https://www.drdansiegel.com/about/interpersonal_neurobiology/

134. Brown, B. (2010, June). *The power of vulnerability.* TED Talks. https://www.ted.com/talks/brene_brown_the_power_of_vulnerability

135. Brown, B. (2012, February). *Listening to shame.* TED Talks. https://www.ted.com/talks/brene_brown_listening_to_shame

239

136. Edmondson, A. (1999). Psychological Safety and Learning Behavior in Work Teams. *Administrative Science Quarterly*, *44*(2), 350. https://doi.org/10.2307/2666999

137. Edmondson, A. C. (2018). *The Fearless Organization: Creating Psychological Safety in the Workplace for Learning, Innovation, and Growth* (1st ed.). Wiley.

138. Google. (n.d.). *re:Work*. https://rework.withgoogle.com/print/guides/5721312655835136/

139. Dewey, J. (1910). *How We Think*. Independently published.

www.ingramcontent.com/pod-product-compliance
Lightning Source LLC
Chambersburg PA
CBHW070306200326
41518CB00010B/1914